GHOST TOWNS

of

WYOMING

GHOST TOWNS
of
WYOMING

by Bruce A. Raisch

The Donning Company Publishers
184 Business Park Drive, Suite 206
Virginia Beach, VA 23462

Steve Mull, General Manager
Barbara Buchanan, Office Manager
Pamela Koch, Editor
Amanda Guilmain, Graphic Designer
Amy Thomann, Imaging Artist
Scott Rule, Director of Marketing
Stephanie Linneman, Marketing Coordinator

Carey Southwell, Project Director

Library of Congress Cataloging-in-Publication Data

Raisch, Bruce A., 1956-
    Ghost towns of Wyoming / by Bruce A. Raisch.
       p. cm.
    Includes bibliographical references.
    ISBN-13: 978-1-57864-352-3 (soft cover : alk. paper)
    ISBN-10: 1-57864-352-X (soft cover : alk. paper)
    1. Ghost towns--Wyoming. 2. Ghost towns--Wyoming--Pictorial
works. 3. Wyoming--History, Local. 4. Wyoming--History, Local
--Pictorial works.   I. Title.
F762.R35 2006
978.7--dc22
                                                        2005035805

Printed in the United States of America at Walsworth Publishing
Company

DEDICATION

I wish to dedicate this book to my father, William A. Raisch. He
instilled in me a love for many things, such as history, maps, the
outdoors, reading, and travel. These gifts have enriched my life and

ACKNOWLEDGMENTS

In addition to the research, this book is the product of seven round-trip drives, seven-thousand-plus road miles, numerous flat tires, and three animal wildlife attacks. All in all though, it was a labor of love, and it is not unusual that there are many to acknowledge and thank.

The Bureau of Land Management, the National Park Service, and the USDA Forest Service, particularly Sharon at the Black Hills headquarters, were all very helpful and a pleasure to deal with. In Wyoming, the State Historical Society and the Departments of Fish and Game, Parks, and Transportation all deserve mention and praise. Especially important was all the help given by Beth Miller of the State of Wyoming, Department of State Parks & Cultural Resources, Customer Service & Outreach, Arts, Parks and History Store.

The little museums at such places as Encampment, Medicine Bow, and Rock River were invaluable. Here, I spent hours pouring over research material. Staff members at these places were eager to help. These are establishments that warrant a visit and deserve your support. The knowledge and willing assistance given to strangers by the "Mayors" of such places like Buford was a pleasant surprise. There was a lot of Western hospitality shown throughout this great state. The people of Wyoming on the whole were helpful and very friendly. A wonderful example of this is Mr. Jesus J. Rodriguez, who spent most of a day giving me a personal tour of the town sites of Hartville and Sunrise, Wyoming.

I would like to give special thanks to Lori. The advice given was more than helpful. Her willingness to give so much of her own time to a project of someone else's shows this to be a giving and generous person. Also I would like to thank my mother for introducing me to Lori.

Last but definitely not least, I must thank Patricia Cracchiola. This adventuress helped with research and typing and actually joined me on several trips. Always there to give one inspiration, she never lost faith in this project or me.

WHAT IS
a ghost town?

Throughout dictionary defines ghost as "a shadowy resemblance of its former self." When you say the phrase "ghost town" for many, a stark Western frontier image usually pops into one's mind—something along the lines of a Hollywood movie set from a John Ford film. True enough, there used to be many such locations, and they were often used by Hollywood as movie sets. Now, most are gone or are mere shadows of even their recent past.

These are fragile things often in harsh places. Some ghost towns have disappeared in the blink of an eye because of landslides or avalanches. Many have burned up in forest fires or have been torched by arsonists. In fact, more mining towns of the Old West burned at least once while occupied. Most of Bodie, California, one of the best ghost towns, was lost to children playing with matches. These wooden towns had burned quite easily when occupied; now they are dried timber boxes. Each sweep of the fire season takes its

Even though completely surrounded by the trees of a national forest, some clueless person decided to use lumber from a 120-year-old building for firewood. Unfortunately, I see this quite frequently.

toll on history. To begin with, sites weren't selected for sustainability. Often, they were above the timberline or had no water source.

While they existed, these places were often miniature hells on earth. Numerous belching stacks pouring forth unfiltered toxins replaced the trees. For example, in Butte, Montana, fumes killed the trees and darkened the skies at noon. Mines were sweltering hotboxes, often above one hundred degrees; the miners died from fire, explosions, falls, deadly gases, and silicosis. No Smoking signs were posted in twenty or more languages. But that mattered little; many miners couldn't read at all.

Danger lurks in many forms for ghost towns, mostly human. For centuries, man has built simply by tearing down an existing structure and using the material to build a new structure. Farmers did this to Roman ruins to build their field fences. The Catholic Church did this to Indian pyramids in Latin America to build their churches. Many an old weather-beaten Western mining town has been liberated of its material or even whole structures. In the American West, ranchers have taken buildings from abandoned towns and ranches to use for another purpose at another location. They still do this today.

The end of World War II and the introduction of the jeep opened many a ghost town in the West and doomed just as many. Mining companies, the Forest Service, and the Bureau of Land Management (BLM) all have leveled whole town sites. They do this in self-defense in today's lawsuit-happy environment. In some cases, the government has even had these locations bulldozed and seeded as "Superfund" clean-up sites. The National Park Service gave this treatment to one extraordinary double site in a small river canyon in Missouri. The location could only be reached by canoe or 4x4 and consisted of a dude ranch on one hill and an old resort on another divided by a beautiful Ozark stream.

Often ghost towns just leave, disappearing one board at a time. Tourists take boards as souvenirs or to make picture frames. A whole building will disappear in this manner in a single season. Sometimes, buildings are taken from one ghost town to another for the benefit of tourists. In some cases, whole tourist ghost towns have been invented and then constructed with the buildings taken from real locations.

There are numerous sources from which to glean ghost town locations. There are many books on the subject, but quite often the information is dated. Always check the publishing date. The Internet will supply you with a list of names that can seem never-ending, but when you read the bios provided, the majority of the time they will say "no remains." Hardly a ghost town then. Also, the information is not necessarily as up-to-date as one would expect in the computer age or as reliable as one would want.

State highway maps often have some locations marked. This almost guarantees you'll have company. The Nevada State Highway map shows thirty-two locations and denotes them with the word "site." This is just a fraction of that state's total ghost town locations. Road atlases provide some locations, but often they seem to duplicate listings found in some of the most dated books, and the sites may be marked only in a general manner. This does not make them easy to find. U.S. geological topographic maps show many locations, but you may need a hundred maps to cover a state. Again, the information may be old; check the date on the bottom of the map. Some maps have not been updated for decades. This can help you with the history of the town, but just because you see it on the map, don't expect to see it at the site. Forest Service maps identify some by putting the name in red letters and the words "ghost town" in bold print next to it. They even have an arrow pointing to the spot. That is pretty definitive.

Comparing new state highway maps with old ones will yield many precise locations to check out. If a highway map from 1980 shows a town at a certain point but your 2002 map doesn't, you may just have found a ghost town. I have found ghost town locations on numerous tourist brochures, motel chain highway maps, and even restaurant paper placemats. I use all available sources and then cross-reference them. When you drive in the West, you may just run into some of them that didn't appear in any of the sources. Often, these are the best locations because they are newer and have not been trampled by a stampede of tourists.

Just as there are many ways to find ghost town sites, there are many different types to find. To start, not all were mining towns. Many were born as farm, railroad, timber, or tourist towns. Some were even CCC (Civilian Conservation Corps) camps. These towns come in all shapes, sizes, and ages. It is not all that uncommon to find abandoned communities from the 1970s and 1980s! Even if it was a mining community, it wasn't always gold or silver that drew the prospector's pick. Mineral wealth also came in the form of coal, cobalt, copper, iron ore, lead, manganese, oil, tin, tungsten, or more. With the end of WWII and the wholesale expansion of the U.S. Armed Forces' nuclear weapons programs, multiple uranium mining towns sprang up. Some of these have now joined the ranks of places that history has passed by.

Often a source, such as the Internet or some book, will list an existing city, such as Butte, Montana, as a ghost town. These communities have much to offer but can hardly be considered ghost towns. If a drop in an area's population and the existence of abandoned buildings within its boundaries qualifies for ghost town status, then many an American inner city would have to be added to the roll call.

On other occasions, the site listed turns out to be a single building, some debris, or even just a sign. Some were never towns but only mining camps, that is, a mine and some miners' cabins without any business or service attached. Some were military posts, deserted Air Force bases, WWII internment camps, or stretches of abandoned railroad sections.

One type of ghost town is the tourist town. As mentioned before, these can be complete fakes. Tourist towns vary greatly in substance although most commonly have admission fees and crowds. Some offer guided tours, and others go further with characters in period costumes who may work at old-time crafts, lead tours, sell cotton candy, or even reenact gunfights. State parks, such as Bodie or Bannack, are some of the best tourist towns. These have rangers instead of reenactors. Here, getting the history right is considered very important.

Some ghost towns were Hollywood movie sets. A movie company could film on a lot or in a studio, but for realism, open country was needed. Once out in the country, the company could either use an existing ghost town or build a set to represent the frontier community. Even when they built film sets, producers often moved buildings from actual ghost towns to get that authentic look. Besides, it was cheaper. Buildings were modified, added, or even destroyed pretty much at will. Some towns, like Paria, Utah, became producer favorites and were used in numerous movies. Today, most of these locations have gone back to ghost status or faded away completely. A few are still used for movies or have been converted into tourist attractions complete with performers reenacting gunfights. These are more amusement parks than ghost towns. They attract crowds, charge admission, and are not necessarily accurate. These tourist Western frontier towns can be found in a number of states from California to Illinois. In fact, a location in Illinois was recently listed for sale on the Internet.

Other locations are classified by sources as living or semi-ghost. People still live at these places but with just a fraction of their former population. They have numerous abandoned buildings, very quiet streets, and few, if any, services. Here, you have the possibility of having your questions answered by the local historian, who is anybody you can find who will talk to you. The local post office, if there is one, is a great place to start. If you decide to "go postal," just be patient and polite. All kidding aside, I have found these people to be pleasant, professional, locally informed, and helpful. Just make sure they are not busy with other customers before cutting into their workday. Remember, a smile will go a long way.

There are "main street" or "business" ghost towns. Most of the housing is occupied, but the majority of the commercial enterprises are vacant.

One thought that pops into the minds of some when they hear the words "ghost town" is a place that is haunted by spirits. This is not what the term means nor does it exclude it. There are some places where a building, a cemetery, or the whole location is believed haunted by one or more "spirits." One more peculiarity of many of these places is the legends of buried treasure and lost mines. Hardly surprising since many were mining towns to begin with. Some locations may be pockmarked with little pits, scars left behind by treasure hunters. The same problem befalls archeological sites, which in themselves are also actually "ghost towns."

Some of these towns only have a single soul living in them, perhaps one who toughs out the winter and lives there year-round. This individual is usually called "the Mayor" and even holds the position officially in a number of cases. Here is a person who, if asked nicely, can often be a wealth of information.

Nearby or within many Western ghost towns is a cemetery. Sometimes, there is a second graveyard, a "Boot Hill." Blacks, Chinese, Indians, and riffraff such as "fancy girls" or horse thieves are buried here. Cemeteries can reveal histories of avalanches, epidemics, mine disasters, and more. There are many books and websites that specialize in cemeteries of the Old West.

When checking out any locations, exercise awareness and caution. Look out for bad road conditions, barbed wire, broken glass, briers, cactus, heatstroke, long distances between services, nails, No Trespassing signs, open vertical shafts, rattlesnakes, and unsafe buildings.

You don't need a license or expensive special equipment to hunt ghost towns, just a sense of adventure and curiosity. To be on the safe side, make sure your vehicle is in good mechanical condition.

Pay special attention to your cooling system, gas gauge, and tires, including your spare. Take a canteen on your hikes and have extra water in your vehicle for both you and the vehicle. Your outfit should include a broad rim hat, good hiking boots, long pants, sunglasses, lip balm, and a walking stick. It is also a good idea to take two cameras; you can take different speed films or color in one and black and white in the other. Last, but not least, take a first aid kit. Road conditions to these towns vary greatly; some can even be dangerous. Good roads are nice, but that means the location is rarely deserted, usually vandalized, and sometimes a tourist trap. To get to some of the best ghost towns, you often have to hike a couple of miles. When you get there, be the good tourist. Ask for directions with a smile and a thank you. Respect property rights. Practice safety for all in your party. Lastly, take nothing but pictures and leave nothing but footprints.

The old frontier mining towns are a vanishing breed from a bygone era. A sense of history hangs in the air of their empty streets. The only sounds that fill your ears are the wind, creaking boards, and the gravel under your boots. They speak to you in silence and reach out to you without hands. In time, you move on but the town can't, for it is frozen in time and has been long passed by.

This book is organized with the sites listed in alphabetical order. The name of the ghost town appears first with the county in which it is located next to it in parentheses, e.g., ADDIE CAMP (Pennington). If I have not physically viewed the location, the term "site not visited" is posted underneath the heading, at the start of the site's bio.

I personally visited the majority of these sites. Even after all the research, there's nothing like viewing the place for yourself; however, this is easier said than done. Many times, the road less traveled or even the trail less hiked was the only way there.

Hazards must be dealt with and permission to visit obtained. A few of the examinations were conducted from a moving vehicle, but the vast majority were boots on! Numerous locations were visited more than once. On occasion, I spent the night in the town and was given a tour or visited the town's museum.

Attention was paid to details, even down to the construction materials used at the sites. The bios that accompany each location are a product of research and my own physical examination of the site.

Of the sites not visited, these are locations that one source or another claims is a ghost town, and research shows they bear interest. There are thirty-five sites, and their history goes back to 1812. Each is accompanied by a historical and physical bio. Without having put my foot on the ground at these places, much information should be considered only my best guess. In all cases, locations of "no remains" will not be listed.

Thanks for your interest, and good hunting.

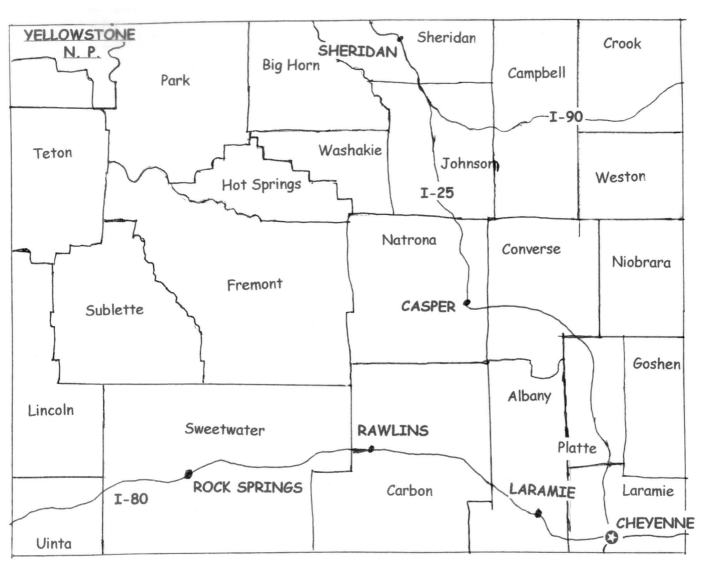

WYOMING

INTRODUCTION

ghost towns of wyoming

W yoming, the Cowboy State, didn't enter the Union until 1890. For decades, it was a place that pioneers and trails passed through on their way to California, Oregon, and the Salt Lake Valley. Among the reasons for this late settlement were hostile Indians, the high altitude, and harsh winters. But the biggest reason was the lack of arable land.

Most of Wyoming is a high altitude desert plateau, sagebrush country. Where pioneers did find trees and water, they also found steep mountains defended by fierce Sioux, Cheyenne, and Arapaho warriors. Fur trappers and prospectors were the first to experience these tough fighters, but things changed with time and with a major force the Indians called the Iron Horse. At the time of the Civil War, rail lines terminated at Kansas City, Missouri. When the war ended, the nation turned its great energy west. Corporate America and the

Even in winter, Yellowstone can be a thing of beauty although to some it may appear as a Nordic netherworld.

Buffalo can be big and beautiful; they can also be dangerous and cause traffic jams.

federal government joined together in the biggest project man had seen to date. Construction of the Continental Railroad brought the Union Pacific thundering across southern Wyoming in 1868. The railroad was the bane of both the buffalo and Indian. It changed the cattle industry, brought in the European wheat farmers, and took out their crops.

With the trains came lumberjacks. The railroads used whole forests for both fuel and railway ties. Buffalo hunters also came with the railroad. Buffalo were the lifeblood of the Plains tribes, and the Indians fought with desperation. They drove the hunters out in 1874, but the hunters returned in a short time accompanied by the U.S. Army. The majority of the buffalo were slaughtered in less than a decade. Next, settlers came. Wheat farmers, cattle ranchers, and saloon owners poured off the trains, which inevitably led to conflict with the current landowners. This in turn led to everyone from railroad executives to ranchers screaming for help from the U.S. government.

The government literally sent in the cavalry. The mission, as the War Department saw it, was to solve the "Indian problem" by pacifying the local indigenous personnel. Pacification meant the reservation or death. The tribes had successfully repelled the first wave of settlement with their victory over the Bozeman Trail and the Fort Laramie Treaty, but the second wave rolled over them. It would take more than a decade, but the Army, prospectors, gold rushes, railroads, and settlers wore the Indians down. Old forts and battle sites dot the historical landscape of this state but for the most part are beyond the scope of this book.

While much of the territory was initially open range for the cattle and sheep ranchers, Wyoming is blessed with an abundance of natural resources. With the railroads and without hostile Indians, miners and prospectors stampeded into the territory. Not only were they seeking the usual gold and silver, but also coal, oil, and timber were high on the list for fortune seekers. Instead of digging up the land, some attempted to get rich "off" the land. Towns sprang up to service all these industries. Uranium and its towns would boom onto the mining list in the next century.

Services on Wyoming back roads are few and far between, if at all.

This is a state of extreme climate, topography, and beauty. Unfortunately, most visitors to this state only view it from either Interstate 80 or Yellowstone National Park. The scenery along I-80 does not allow Wyoming to put its best foot forward and although Yellowstone is a national gem, it is a crowded, expensive, heavily regulated, and traffic-snarled gem. Two mountain island oases, the Medicine Bow and the Big Horn, plus the western edge of the Black Hills interrupt the ruggedly beautiful high plain of Wyoming. The desert blazes during summer and snow falls in the mountains even in August. Winters can be brutal all over the state. This is definitely a place for the lover of the great outdoors.

Ghost town locations are often found grouped together in clumps around the site of a major mining strike. When someone located gold or another metal ore in a mountain range, a cluster of towns soon popped up around the discovery as happened in Wyoming at the Medicine Bow and Big Horn mountains. Abandoned towns may also be found strung along old highways and railroad right-of-ways

like pearls on a strand. The old Lincoln Highway is a great example of this in the Cowboy State. When these routes shut down, so goes the lifeblood of these communities.

When not traveling on the Interstate, it can be a long distance between services. Water is scarce. Winters are harsh. High winds with drifting snow cause a hazard called "ground blizzards." These winds produce a wind-chill factor that is more than just dangerous—it can be deadly. Travel warnings are posted and winter survival tips provided. The best ghost town hunting tip is to stay out of Wyoming during the winter. If you are not convinced about the danger of high altitude and off-road Western winter travel, just check out the history of Alfred Packer or the Donner Party.

If you do decide to travel the Wyoming backcountry, pack an emergency road kit with a blanket, Fix-A-Flat®, flares, a flashlight, a first aid kit, matches, motor oil, antifreeze, duct tape, a tire tool, a shovel, extra food, and water. If you are camping, you should have most of this gear with you to begin with. Try to wait out bad weather. The wind and low humidity here can quickly dry out dirt roads. Fuel your vehicle as often as possible. Frequently, it can be a good distance between gas stations in this state. You could carry extra fuel, but this too can be a hazard.

Consider the altitude when hiking. Also, take a hiking stick and watch for snakes. At restaurant stops, vegetables are often scarce. I once asked a waitress if the establishment had a vegetable, and she replied, "potatoes are on the menu." On the other hand, the steaks are usually excellent.

A few helpful road notes: Road signs on secondary highways are ventilated from frequent use as targets for marksmanship practice. Just because a map shows a town, it doesn't guarantee any services are there. Rand McNally and AAA road atlases frequently show ghost towns that no longer exist.

Top: Stuck in the Savage Wilderness Area during late June. Snow can be a hazard on the back roads twelve months out of the year in Wyoming.

Bottom: Be bear aware and follow all safety rules.

A herd of moose photographed at 6:00 a.m. in the Big Horn Mountains. These large creatures are beautiful but also dangerous. Do not approach.

Any locations mentioned in books, websites, etc., that were listed as "no remains" have been intentionally omitted from this book. To the best of my knowledge, the seventy-four locations that follow this introduction are all the ghosts with remains contained in the state of Wyoming. I have poured years of research and seven trips to Wyoming into this production. Still, considering the nature and scope of this work, I would not be surprised to learn that I missed some locations during my search. Numerous named sites appear in certain atlases that do not appear on recent road maps of the state. This does not necessarily mean they are or were towns. They may have been section houses, railroad sidings, or water tank locations. Others are oil fields, ranches, or watering holes. If they ever were towns, many were so small as to be of no consequence. These locations appear on no website or in any book I could find, but that does not preclude that some of them are undiscovered ghosts. Also, a number of the sites that are contained in this body of work may have since succumbed to avalanche, fire, or the bulldozer.

WYOMING

ghost town sites

SITES VISITED

Atlantic City
Bald Mountain City
Battle
Bosler
Bryan
Buford
Cambria
Carbon Timber Town
Coyote Springs
Fort Fred Steele State Historical Site
Fort Steele
Hartville
Heart Mountain Relocation Camp
Hecla
Inyan Kara
Jay Em
Jeffrey City
Keystone
Manville
McFadden
Medicine Bow
Mineral Hill
Monarch
Moskee
Opal
Piedmont
Rambler
Reliance
Rock River
Sage
Shell
South Pass City
Sunrise
Superior
Tinton
Tubb Town/Field City
Vacation Ranch
Walcott
Welcome

SITES NOT VISITED

Acme
Antelope Flats
Bessemer Bend
Bitter Creek
Border
Carbon
Copperton
Crosby
Cumberland
Dillon
Dines
Duncan, The
Dunn
Eadsville
East Plane
Gebo
Gillespie Place/Radium Hot Springs
Gunn
Jelm
Kirwin
Lavoye
Lee City
Lewiston
Milford/North Fork
Miners Delight/Hamilton City
Old Upton/Iron Town
Pacific Springs
Rock Creek
Rudefeha
Silver Cliff/New Rochelle/Running Water
Silver Crown
Stansbury
Sublette
Trailtown
Winton

WYOMING

ghost towns

ACME (Sheridan)
SITE NOT VISITED

A once-booming coal mining community, this town thrived at the
same time as neighboring communities Kleenburn and Monarch.
Acme is shown on the official Wyoming State Highway map.
Remains reportedly are a bridge, a cemetery, an old power plant, and
some foundations. The site is a few miles east of I-90 at exit #14.

ANTELOPE FLATS (Teton)
SITE NOT VISITED

Reportedly, only a barn is left. It is on a popular mountain bike route
and said to offer the Tetons as a beautiful photographic backdrop.

Established as a farm community by pioneers from Kansas in 1893,
the town was deserted in 1912 because of repeated crop failure
brought on by cold weather and high altitude. Antelope Flats is
about thirteen miles east of Jackson on a four-wheel-drive road.

The environment around Atlantic City is beautiful and, at the same time, harsh. Carry
extra water and travel the area only during good weather.

ATLANTIC CITY (Fremont)

This place and its sister community, South Pass City, are probably Wyoming's best-known ghost towns. They began in a very typical manner: a gold rush. These towns were nearly twins, both gold mining centers. They were about the same size, in the same geographic area, and followed the same boom-and-bust cycle. Atlantic City, however, was a wild frontier town, and South Pass City was tamer and more family-oriented.

Atlantic City was one of a number of mining camps that were outgrowths of nearby booming South Pass City. Several miners from South Pass on a trip of unknown purpose accidentally discovered gold near Rock Creek during the summer of 1868. They found a vein of gold-bearing quartz several feet thick and thousands of feet long called the "Atlantic Ledge." It slanted sharply at an angle into the ground, but this didn't stop mineshafts from following by the dozen. Three men named Collins, Thompson, and Tozier immediately started a town.

Timber was scarce, the environment was harsh, water was hard to come by except during flash floods, Indian attacks were frequent, and the nearest railhead was a hundred miles away; but still gold fever kept the "rushers" coming. It is claimed that the town grew to a population of two thousand by 1870, but one printed census disputes that number.

The town had a church, livery, beer garden, dance hall, newspaper, and the territory's first brewery. One building, two-story and constructed of stone, was used as a general store on the first floor and as a dance hall on the second floor. It is said that Calamity Jane lived in Atlantic City for a while and ran the dance hall. A minor earthquake has since reduced the building to one story. The town operated a couple of dozen stamp mills for the gold mines in the area. The mills had to be hauled over land through a hundred miles of wilderness, from the Union Pacific rail line in the south.

This first rush lasted ten years until 1878—a long time compared to many mining camps. However, a number of the original mines stayed open, albeit on a limited scale, until 1920.

The next surge of activity came during 1882 in the form of a French engineer named Emil Granier. He arrived in town with foreign capital and a plan to bring water to the gold fields of the Atlantic Ledge. With three hundred Swedish laborers, he built a twenty-mile ditch from Christina Lake in the northern watershed to Atlantic City. The canal was cut through miles of solid rock. Numerous wooden sluices were built to bridge the canyons and gullies encountered en route. Once the canal reached Atlantic City, it followed the land contours and circled half the town. A dam was constructed on the creek that flowed out of Christina Lake.

The project was appropriately called the Christina Ditch. Granier had as his chief engineer one W. G. Peters. It appears he needed a better engineer. The grade for the ditch had been laid out with too much slope, and the sluice boxes were poorly constructed. When the gates at the Christina Lake Dam were opened, the water rushed downgrade too fast. The sluices couldn't take the sudden pressure, and many were wiped out. It was a disaster for Emil Granier and his investors but a temporary bonanza for many local miners. Miners rushed in from all over the area and used the water for panning. In many gullies, minor surface strikes were made. This led to a boom for many a local saloon owner. Emil Granier, now broke, returned to France to try to explain to his investors and to try to refinance the operation. Instead, he was arrested, jailed, tried, convicted, and sentenced to life in prison, where he died a few years later.

Still, some small miners and prospectors hung on. Occasionally, a new store or hotel was built. A black-and-white photo from 1906 shows about forty buildings running down both sides of a gully. During 1912, the town's famous log church was built. It is now a registered national landmark.

By 1920, the last of the mines closed. The next surge of activity came during the Depression. During 1933, a company named E. T. Fisher built and operated a mining dredge on the streams near Atlantic City. It was a massive traveling mill mounted on rails but needed only two men to operate it. The mill, which operated on Rock Creek, would draw up the gravel and sand in front of it and by conveyor belt carry it up to the gold washer. Here, the gold was separated, and the tailings were deposited behind the mill. The mill would literally inch down the creek; the rails in the back were moved to the front to continue the process. At least ten miles of Rock Creek was dredged, and over $700,000 in gold recovered. This does not mean there was a profit; dredging operations required a great deal of capital. The dredging operation also destroys a creek in the process, leaving nothing behind but sterile gravel tailings.

The operation lasted only a couple of years. Ruins of the dredge are still in Rock Creek. But this is a town with more lives than a cat. In 1962, the United States Steel Corporation started a surface iron ore mining operation with modern extraction facilities. It was about three miles north of Atlantic City but closed in 1982.

Next, it started to serve tourists that wanted to see an Old West ghost town. Although a number of sources claimed the town catered to tourists, when I drove through it in 2001, I noticed no businesses in the town. It had become a cottage community. Many are summer residents; others are full-time prospectors. Most of the buildings are completely rehabbed, but some false fronts and wooden boardwalks may still be seen. The church on the hill still holds occasional services.

The turnoff to Atlantic City is twenty-seven miles south of Lander, Wyoming, and is well marked. You take a left and head about five miles east on a good gravel road. Historic South Pass City is four and a half miles southwest. Stay on the marked road unless you have a detailed area map and you are a good map-reader. It is a spider web of dirt roads leading in all directions. Rusting mining equipment and old frontier debris dot the landscape. There are a number of intact mines that surround the town awaiting possible reactivation. One, the Rose Mine, has been in operation off and on for over a hundred years. Its initial vein was rich, but it's been slim diggings since. Other intact mines here are the Diana, Caribou, Garfield, Mingsolomon, and Tabor.

If you have time, visit the ruins of the old gold washer on Rock Creek, a few miles downstream from the town.

BALD MOUNTAIN CITY (Sheridan)

There is not much to view. The only remains are scrap metal and rotten timbers that were log foundations. Trees have grown in clumps where some of the buildings were located. There is a single, roofless, shoulder-high, rough log structure. It shows that what little construction there was here was primitive even by the standards of its day. Bald Mountain City is listed on many atlases, books, highway maps, and websites but hardly worth a visit. Your time would be better spent seeing the Medicine Wheel National Historic site, which is just a few miles west. Both of these places are in the Bighorn National Forest on the north side of Highway 14A. Because

Above: There is so little to see or photograph at Bald Mountain City, so I recommend that one visit the nearby Medicine Wheel instead. This is an archeological site that is as interesting as it is mystifying.

Left: Bald Mountain lent its name to the nearby gold mining community of Bald Mountain City.

of snow, the area is impassable in winter. It has typical mountain weather—it can change in a minute and is quite windy. Altitude is about nine thousand feet. It wasn't an easy place for the miners to live. Many didn't stay during the winter season.

Fine-grained gold was discovered just north of Bald Mountain in 1890. Prospectors moved into the area between Porcupine Creek and the headwaters of the Little Horn River. Things took off in 1892 when a corporation named the Fortunates Mining and Milling Company bought up many of the claims in the area. The increased activity led to the birth of Bald Mountain City. It is located by Porcupine Creek just north of Bald Mountain and was the largest settlement in the Big Horn Mountains at that time.

The majority of the place was a tent city, but since it wasn't above the tree line, a number of log buildings were constructed. These are the remains you see today, barely. There was a newspaper and many saloons but no church. The mining method was panning, and things didn't pan out. Miners tried for ten years, but no mother lode was found. In 1900, the town died.

This is the last intact original structure from the copper mining town of Battle.

The best place to find the history of the town of Battle or to see its artifacts, like this ore bucket, is the museum in the town of Encampment.

BATTLE (Carbon)

This is a location shown on many maps and road atlases. Signs on the highway direct you to Battle, but you find there isn't much to see. The site consists of a rest area, a couple of plaques, a roofless log cabin, the wood foundations of two more buildings, and not much else. Part of the town site was hauled away to the museum in Encampment. There was a cemetery from the boom days, but I did not locate it. Still, Battle is the easiest, if not the best, of a small group of boomers to visit. There are not many intact structures at any of these locations anymore. Summer cottages of various descriptions occupy a good portion of the old site of Battle. Some are old homes of Battle completely rehabbed, others are brand new, and a third type appear constructed with elements of every decade since the community was found. The CCC intentionally burned down some structures in 1933 when the site was converted to a campground.

Battle, which got its start in 1898, was also called Portland for a while. Its existence was mostly due to the copper boom in the area,

This part of the original tramway that carried copper ore out of Medicine Bow Mountains to the smelter in Encampment can be seen at the museum in Encampment.

but it also was a frontier town that serviced the cattlemen, loggers, and sheepherders. Sheepmen were the source of several gunfights in town; miners and cattlemen were competing with them for the same land. The town was named after nearby Battle Pass, which got its name, very appropriately, from a battle fought there. Twenty-three trappers from the Rocky Mountain Fur Company had more than a slight disagreement with an estimated five hundred Arapaho, Cheyenne, and Sioux warriors. The conflict with the Plains Indians, the rugged terrain, and the harsh mountain winters kept this area from being settled by the white man as quickly as it might. The first prospectors here carried firearms for protection against Indian attack.

Rudefeha, not Battle, was the name of the mine that operated here. Curiously, Battle Mine was more than a dozen miles away at the town of Rudefeha. The Rudefeha got its name from an amalgamation of the names of the investors: J. M. Rusmey, Robert Deal, George Ferris, and Ed Haggarty.

Winters can be harsh with heavy snow. This same snow can and often did close Battle Pass. The high altitude contributed to hard living conditions. It was 9,873 feet at the town of Battle, 9,915 feet at the Pass. The Continental Divide runs down the spine of the Medicine Bow Mountains, forming the Sierra Madre Range. Winter snows would cut the towns apart or even isolate them completely.

Many would spend winters at a lower altitude in nearby Encampment or Riverside. Encampment was also the site of the smelter where copper-bearing ore was sent by wagon or mule train, at first. The area is too steep and rugged for even a narrow-gauge train. The train did run to Encampment by 1908.

An aerial tramway was built at great expense. At the time, it was the longest in the world. The tramway was fourteen miles long, used 985 buckets, rested on 304 towers, and moved at four miles per hour. Later, the length was increased to twenty miles. Each bucket could hold seven hundred pounds of ore, and it supposedly could deliver a total of ninety-eight tons daily. It took the copper ore from the Rudefeha Mine in Battle to the smelter in Encampment where today a museum offers displays of the process. The tramway was completed in 1902, but the first ore wasn't delivered until June 1903. Other mines, such as the Rambler, probably used the tramway too. It's only logical. The same men owned the Battle, Rambler, Rudefeha, and many other mines. Whatever they charged independent miners would have been less expensive than hauling out ore by mule train.

The copper boom here lasted from 1897 to 1908 when the last mines closed. Battle lasted as a town until 1911. There were problems with fires—forest, mine, and even the smelter twice (at Encampment). Production costs per ton were high, and the price of copper dropped 35 percent in 1907. Copper discovered in Montana was available in large quantities and cheaper to mine. This plus the end of the Spanish-American War caused copper prices to plunge. Then, the company was indicted for stock fraud. They had severely overcapitalized. A court found them guilty of fraudulent stock sales. This was the death of the mines of the Sierra Madre. Production ended even though the copper veins had not played out.

Most of the mining operation was up along Haggarty Creek, but others, such as Rambler, ran along the Continental Divide. No mother lode was ever found. The other towns of the boom were Copperton, Dillon, Elwood, Hog Park, Rambler, and Rudefeha. At its peak, Battle had a population of 250 plus. The town had five saloons, a general store, a land sales office, a barbershop, a feed stable, a lumber company, a school, two hotels, restaurants, boarding houses, and a newspaper, the *Battle Lake Miner*. Today, the most it offers is a nice rest stop on State Highway 70.

A final note and all too common in the West: When the Rudefeha Mine was closed, the shafts were sealed with no provision made for drainage. Of course, over time, the shafts flooded, became polluted with heavy metals, and seeped into otherwise pristine mountain streams. Often in the early mining West, no regard was given to the environment or the future. The worst examples were hydraulic and dredge mining operations. At the same time, however, other visionaries created the likes of Yellowstone and Yosemite national parks.

BESSEMER BEND (Natrona)
SITE NOT VISITED

This is a Bureau of Land Management interpretive site with six plaques. It is located at the Bessemer Bend of the North Platte River. There is much history here and Bessemer shows on a number of atlases as a ghost town, but I believe the BLM signs to be the only things to see.

United States history starts early for Bessemer Bend. In November 1812, a fur trading party led by Robert Stuart built a cabin south of here. It was supposedly the first European-type structure built in Wyoming. Later, the Mormon and Oregon trails would pass through and follow the river for hundreds of miles. Early emigrants would cross the river here. Farther upstream, the North Platte turns south and becomes swifter, rendering it impassable for such wagon traffic.

After 1847, a number of toll bridges and ferries crossed the river downstream of the Bend. Many emigrants, including the Mormon Handcart Companies of 1856, couldn't or wouldn't pay these tolls. Instead, they used the crossing at Bessemer during low water. At this time, travelers also called this place Red Buttes after the rock formations that stand above the area. A small settlement began to provide services for the numerous travelers. This location was also used as a stop on the pony express mail route and a stagecoach line.

Natrona County was established in 1890. An election was held to see which town, Bessemer or Casper, would become the county seat. Casper won a disputed election. In fact, there was some speculation that Casper stole the election. Bessemer Bend went downhill from there. Roads that replaced pioneer trails bypassed the place, and Bessemer faded from the maps and Wyoming.

Many road atlases report this as a ghost town location and even show it in two different places. One location is on the west side of Wyoming Highway 220; the other is nearby on the east side of the highway. To find the correct west side location, head northwest for six miles on Highway 220.

Near mile marker 106, you'll see a sign for Bessemer Bend (County Road 308). Follow this road for one and a half miles, turn right at an intersection, and then continue to the bridge. The interpretive site is on the opposite side. It is open daily, and there is no fee. I do not know if there are any other remains.

BITTER CREEK (Sweetwater)
SITE NOT VISITED

A small section town founded by the Union Pacific Railroad, Bitter Creek lasted as a water tank and whistle stop for decades. Its need faded with the end of steam power. The location is still marked on most highway maps and atlases.

Remains are said to be one old intact building, a dilapidated water tank, and a small number of foundations.

Bitter Creek is located nine miles south of I-80 from exit #142 on Bitter Creek Road. An interstate rest stop is located a few miles east of this exit.

BORDER (Lincoln)
SITE NOT VISITED

This is a small, late-twentieth-century, highway ghost town. I drove through the spot but did not stop to investigate the site. The town has had two locations. Originally, this was a Union Pacific water tank town. The first town site of Border should be around two to three miles south of the intersection of highways 30 and 89. Trains no longer stop at the first location although it still shows on most maps or atlases, including the state highway map. Remains there, if any, are unknown to me. None were visible from the highway. When the highway intersection was built, a new town of Border was born. Most of the business and population probably moved from the original Border, a declining railroad location, to the hopeful promise of the modern-day highway.

The present location of Border is scattered over a large area. Some buildings are abandoned; others just look that way. Most construction near the intersection is from the late twentieth century, but older structures are visible in the desert. One vacant business was being used as a seasonal fireworks stand while others were occupied by squatters. There is also a vacated highway maintenance building and yard at this site. For a couple of decades, farms have consolidated and increased in size, creating vacant farmsteads. These vacant farm and ranch buildings extend south of the town for a few miles.

The Bosler school, grades kindergarten through twelve.

The location on the Idaho–Wyoming state border is the obvious origin of the community's name. The environment here is that of a hot desert plateau.

BOSLER (Albany)

Bosler is one of many ghost towns that dot the old Lincoln Highway, U.S. 30/Highway 287; in fact, the road bisects the community. When the Interstate was built, it followed a straighter and more southerly route, taking most of the road traffic with it. Bosler was also once a railroad stop, but the depot went out of use.

A pair of websites mentioned a post office and a furniture store called "Doc's" as the last entities still operating in this town. Both were closed during my visit in the summer of 2002. The websites also claimed a population of fifteen. That estimate appeared to be a little high. I found an abandoned two-story, yellow, brick school building and library in very good condition and a very old motor motel that appears to be from the 1930s. There are about five other abandoned businesses along with about eight derelict houses and one mobile home out of use. A small number of vacant buildings and homes belonging to abandoned ranchers dot the horizon. There are occupied residences together with a few vacant ones on the south side of the railroad tracks.

This town also has a number of abandoned vehicles, some dating to the 1930s. The derelict cars, trucks, and vans outnumber the buildings. This place is windy and subjected to snowdrifts in the winter. Elevation is 7,074 feet. Farther west on this route, you will find the ghost towns of Rock River, Medicine Bow, and Walcott.

BRYAN (Sweetwater)

Bryan was a Union Pacific railroad town founded in 1868 that also served as a freight wagon center and a stagecoach stop. Some thought Bryan would become a communications hub, but it never came to pass. A better place for the terminal was a town/ferry crossing called Green River.

Top: The remains of an older motor court from the 1920s or 1930s.

Middle: Doc's Furniture Store was the last open business establishment in this town. Although now closed, numerous websites still incorrectly list this store as open.

Bottom: Men's and women's restrooms for a business establishment that is no longer standing.

Top: Highway 30, the old Lincoln Highway, bisects the town of Bosler.

Bottom: Numerous abandoned and vintage autos dot the landscape here.

At that time, the railroads needed water even more than fuel to keep their steam locomotives puffing along, and the Green River had a lot more water than Black Forks that flowed past Bryan. But one S. I. Fields owned the land rights in the area. So the Union Pacific established their headquarters, terminal, and a twelve-stall roundhouse for the area in Bryan. Huge quantities of goods shipped here by rail were loaded onto freight wagons and then hauled to the South Pass mining district.

Bryan was presumably lively and somewhat rough, with law administered by vigilante justice. The majority of the houses were situated between the railroad and Black Forks. Most homes were logs and planks on the bottom half and tent canvas on the top half although there were some buildings of more substantial construction. For instance, there was a bank and the two-story Martin's Hotel. Bryan was also a hauling point for freight wagons. It is reported that, at its peak, Bryan had a population of five thousand, but this seems high.

Things changed in a hurry. S. I. Fields sold his land rights, and the Black Forks went dry. So in 1872, the Union Pacific moved the terminal to Green River after all. Moreover, at the same time, the gold rush at South Pass had dried up. Bryan shrank drastically overnight but did not die. It was still there as a community at least until 1931. The location is on County Road 41, twelve miles west of the Green River and four miles north of I-80. This road is somewhat rough and should be traveled only in dry weather. The actual town is situated partially on a railroad right-of-way and partially on private ranch property.

Remains here are scant. They consist of a few sheds and old railroad cars converted into various buildings. Some foundations from the roundhouse may exist in the sage scrub. A cemetery is about a quarter of a mile from the present remains of Bryan on a low, scrub-covered hill. It overlooks both the old town site and Black Forks. A historical marker is one mile south on State Highway 374. Numerous highway atlases show this spot as the ghost town location.

BUFORD (Albany)

This is a very little town with a lot of history. Buford is shown on all maps and atlases of Wyoming. A billboard on I-80 brags of the town's historic past. Postcards have been printed of this place, and interstate highway signs tell you of its approach—all for a very friendly population of two.

Top: There are numerous vacant homes whose construction spans from the 1920s to the 1960s at Bosler.

Bottom: When you follow maps to the site of Bryan, all you find is this sign. The actual location of Bryan is one mile north in the desert and only consists of a few sheds and a cemetery.

There is very little to see here, but it is a good information and supply stop.

Buford got its start as Fort Sanders in 1866. During 1869, the Union Pacific built a siding and shipping depot at the spot, used mainly for timber and cattle. It is said that Republican President Grant passed through the town that year, but this is unconfirmed. It is also alleged that Butch Cassidy committed a robbery here. This was the first railroad stop entering Albany County from the east. During 1880, the fort was renamed Fort Buford after General John Buford.

Fort Sanders/Buford was the county seat for Laramie County until it moved to Cheyenne in 1886. When the fort closed, Buford became a trading post and rail stop. A small town complete with a school grew slowly. For a while, this was a railroad section town. The Union Pacific would set up housing about every five miles for its workers who would maintain that section of track. Hence the name "section town." Since this location had businesses and a school, a larger-than-average section housing unit was built. Buford never grew to a large size and slowly faded back into the prairie. Union Pacific removed its housing sections between 1982 and 1989. The trading post became a gas station/store. Its owner has converted some of the old structures for current use.

The 1905 school is now a workshop, an 1895 store is now a garage, and one of the original cabins is used as a shed. The only other structures are the gas station/store known as the "Trading Post" and the owner's home. The owner is the unofficial mayor of this unincorporated community. This location is a good stop for gas, snacks, drinks, directions, and local history. The "Mayor" is friendly and eager to be of help. Nearby are the locations of Sherman and Hecla. [Author's note: In a follow-up telephone call, I learned that the "Trading Post" had burned down in mid-August 2003. The owner, regretfully, was unsure if or when this historical business might reopen. A drive-by on my 2005 visit revealed that it had been rebuilt and is again open to the public.]

This site is located on the south side of I-80 at exit #335. At an elevation of eight thousand feet, Buford claims it is the highest town between New York City and San Francisco. It even has its own postcard extolling this claim. While it's not actually the highest town in the United States or even on an interstate, it is the highest community on I-80, which connects San Francisco with New York City.

CAMBRIA (Weston)

Because, technically, there are three different Cambrias, much conflicting information is written about this town, and it is even shown on maps at different locations. The first of the three sites was a salt mine, a very valuable commodity in the pioneer days of the Black Hills. Salt was used in bulk to process food or hides and to preserve food. It was also used in medicine and, most importantly, in mining for chloridizing gold and silver ore. In the beginning of the Black Hills mining rush, the nearest railroad was almost two hundred miles away. Freight costs for hauling even such a simple thing as salt were extremely expensive for the mines. Europeans looked for and found salt springs at the head of Salt Creek Canyon on July 8, 1877. Salt Creek was already known in the area, and it was as simple as following it upstream. Even today, the chloride is easily visible as white patches on the bottom of the canyon.

In November 1878, James LeGraves came to the salt springs to start a salt processing operation. During the next six years, LeGraves produced salt during the summer months by the simple means of evaporation. Most of the salt went to the mines, but some went to the general stores in Deadwood and Lead. In 1904, N. H. Darton issued a promising report stating that the spring here discharged about thirty-five thousand pounds of salt a day. The water discharge is a little more than 5 percent salt in content.

Even with an expanded rail network, the western markets needed Cambria's salt. In 1907, an investment group, encouraged by the Darton report, committed a large amount of capital to expand the salt operation. It was known as the Cambria Salt Company. Brine was pumped about ten miles west to an evaporating and purifying plant near the Cambria Coal Mines. Coal from the Cambria mines was used to fuel the plant. The company unsuccessfully attempted to locate the bed of rock salt from which the brine discharged. At least three wells were drilled, with one as deep as 825 feet. The wells can still be seen here today. The operation was a failure, and the equipment of the Cambria Salt Company was sold at a public bankruptcy sale on May 11, 1909. This ended the "salt" history of

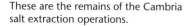

These are the remains of the Cambria salt extraction operations.

Now known as the Flying V Cambria Inn, this structure was formerly called Cambria Casino. The building was originally erected for the miners of the coal town of Cambria.

Cambria. In addition to the wells, the only other remains here are a historical marker, an old wagon road, piping, and some debris.

This Cambria is located north of Newcastle on the east side of Highway 85. There is a second historical marker south of here on the west side of the highway. It gives the history for "coal" Cambria, which is five miles west of the sign—another reason why sources have trouble marking this location.

The coal town of Cambria was founded in 1887 and shut down in 1928 when the coal vein pinched out. At its peak in 1904, the mine employed 550 men, and the town boasted a population of 1,400. Kilpatrick Brothers & Collins, contractors to the railroad, built the towns and operated the mines. This was a company town. The Chicago, Burlington & Quincy Railroad used the coal as fuel for their steam locomotives. There was a large company commissary store where the miners could pay for things with company scrip and other locals could shop with cash. The developers also built a reservoir, a bank, a courthouse, a train depot, an opera house, a school, a lodge hall, a recreation hall, a two-story hotel, two churches, numerous company offices, and over 150 miners' homes. As a company town, there were no saloons or dance halls. The men went to Newcastle for these distractions.

The mine closed at the end of a day's work shift, and the town emptied literally overnight. During breakfast at a nice family café in Newcastle, I was very fortunate to meet the nice lady whose father blew the work whistle that final day. Locals in these communities possess a wealth of historical knowledge and are often eager to share it with you—not unusual in most of Wyoming. During WWII, most of the town was dismantled. Still, many structures were there in the 1970s, which is amazing because this was a place built of wood and surrounded by pine forest—the perfect combination for fire to do its work.

If you include Tinton, Cambria is one of eight Wyoming Black Hills ghosts. Photos dating from the early 1990s show many buildings in good shape. Since then, numerous websites claim all the buildings are gone, and it is not known how, when, or why. Most websites conclude the buildings were likely torn down to avoid liability from trespassers.

One grand building does exist—the Flying V Cambria Inn, the third Cambria. Construction started in 1923 on a resort known as the "Cambria Casino," which was completed in 1928, just as the town was closing down. It was then leased to the Flying V cattle ranch. Later, it operated as a bible camp and then a dude ranch before becoming a bed and breakfast. Today, it is still called the Flying V. There are a small number of frontier buildings on the grounds, but they appear to have been moved to this place. The Cambria Inn itself is a fine stone structure and a national registered landmark. A book on Black Hills ghost towns displays a photo of a three-story frame hotel and refers to it as the Cambria Inn. This is not the Cambria Casino, but rather the original company hotel in the town of Cambria itself. It is now reportedly gone. The Flying V Cambria Inn is located a few miles east of "coal" Cambria on the east side of Highway 85 just north of Newcastle.

After the mines closed, the site was used little. The post office stayed open only until December 31, 1928. The Farm Security

Administration, a New Deal program, occupied one of the abandoned buildings during the 1930s. Local hunters and prospectors freely used the numerous vacant homes.

This is a much-photographed site. The Farm Security Administration took seventy-seven thousand photos from 1935 to 1942 to show the poverty of farmers and migrant workers. Hence, most of the photos are intentionally bleak in appearance.

Northeast of the town, there is a cemetery with many ornate tombstones. Area residents, including those in Newcastle, discourage visits here or to almost any Black Hills ghost. They have had too much trouble with arson, theft, litter, trespassing, vandalism, etc. Too many tourists forget the simple rule: "Take nothing but pictures; leave nothing but footprints."

The coal town of Cambria is located just north of Newcastle, up Cambria Creek, in a small valley. Access to this site is through private property and permission to pass through must be granted, although you are discouraged from even asking. The site itself is also on private property and separate permission must be arranged to visit. Locals say some buildings are still standing here; others collapsed, but most were moved. Coal waste is plentiful at the head of Cambria Canyon. The area's pine forest is still recovering.

CARBON (Carbon)
SITE NOT VISITED

This was a coal-mining town, founded in 1868 by the Union Pacific Railroad to provide fuel for steam locomotives. The first miners in Carbon lived in dugouts in ravines; later, houses were built of sandstone. Water had to be hauled from Medicine Bow. Indian attacks and mining accidents were both frequent and often fatal. At its peak in 1890, there were seven coal mines and claims of between 1,140 and 3,000 residents in Carbon. There was a general store, eight saloons, two churches, a miners' hall, an opera house, a school, a newspaper, a bank, a hotel, and other businesses.

In 1890, a fire destroyed a good portion of the business section. An overturned kerosene lamp ignited the fire in a bunkhouse. Dynamite was used to fight the spread of the fire. During 1899, the mines started to play out, and by 1902, the last one had closed. The rail line was then moved north to an easier grade; this was the final blow. Many of the miners moved to nearby Hanna, even taking a fair number of buildings with them, including the large miners' hall.

This is a windswept location set amongst a maze of four-wheel-drive roads, accessed through private property. After rains, dirt roads turn into seas of mud. The cemetery is supposed to contain some history. The first person buried here died during an Indian attack when the camp was first established. One person was lynched. Most graves are of children or coal miners who died too young. Today, all that remains are foundations, streets, debris, a cemetery, and a historical marker.

CARBON TIMBER TOWN (Carbon)

This may well have been the town with no name; its history is sketchy. It is across the river from a state park (Fort Steele Historical Site), yet the staff knows little of this place. Even locals, when found, only acknowledge its use as a company timber town. This location does not show on modern maps, was found on no websites, and was included in only one book to my knowledge.

This much is known about the spot. A company named the Carbon Timber Company processed timber into lumber. The exact years of operation are unknown to me, but this operation continued to run after the Continental Railroad was built. Timber operations started during 1868. Like a couple of other locations in this part of Wyoming, this was a place where timber was floated downriver from the Medicine Bow Mountains to be converted into railroad ties. The ties were used by the Union Pacific railroad to help construct the transcontinental railroad. I do not know if the Carbon Timber Company was a subsidiary of the Union Pacific Railroad or an independent contractor.

The town rests on the east bank of the North Platte River. An island starts just upstream of the town, dividing the river into two channels. The right side channel is where the timber was recovered from the river. The timber was moved downstream from the lumber camps in drives, much like herding cattle. These drives would consist of up to five hundred thousand logs and cover as much as twenty miles of the river. Dozens of men would ride the logs downstream using long poles much like a riverman on a raft or johnboat. It would take up to two months to herd the timber to the mills downstream. The midway point was the town of Saratoga. Here, the "tie hacks," as these lumber herders were called, would take a drinking break. Sometimes this break would last a week. This was a wet, cold, and dangerous job. Logjams occurred constantly and were unblocked by a man diving under the pile and placing a dynamite charge on the obstruction—extremely dangerous work.

On the other hand, extremely dangerous work was fairly common in the pioneer West. At the end of these drives, the tie hacks were paid, and they usually headed off to the nearest saloon. These

This was a conveyor that transferred timber from the river to the mill.

drives continued until at least 1931. The end of these operations probably wasn't caused by the Depression but by overcutting. Black-and-white photos from 1907 of Medicine Bow towns such as Battle and Rambler show the areas completely denuded of trees. When the timber reached the company town, it was herded into the slower right hand channel and lifted onto three loading ramps that could handle fourteen thousand ties during a nine-hour shift. It doesn't take a math major to figure out what was happening in the mountains: complete deforestation. This site rests on a flood plain, and clearcutting the mountains must have made the flooding situation worse. Numerous boats were used to help corral the timber, but all are long since gone. Most of the timber was milled, but starting in 1929, much was sent to Laramie.

As previously mentioned, this was a company town and as such had company housing. Most of the housing units were bachelor quarters.

This structure housed the steam boiler that provided power for the conveyors and was fueled by wood waste from the operation.

Because of the weather and river levels, it is hard to picture this place as a year-round operation. No tie drives would take place during winter, but there might have been enough backlog of timber to keep the mills running. This probably means that most of the work and population were seasonal.

I explored the site for an hour and did not come close to covering the whole area. There are many trees and much undergrowth that make viewing anything from a distance impossible. I found numerous mill structures and trestles here, all in bad shape, but did not find the "town" part of the location. It may or may not be there now. According to one report, there was a company store. Faintly printed on its false front were the words "Carbon Timber Co. Store Dept."; hence, the name for the town. This location should not be confused with the ghost town of Carbon, a number of miles east in the same county.

There are numerous railroad spurs running over this location, with a number of them running adjacent to the old trestles. These probably operated on the continuous belt system and hauled the timber from the river to the mill or to be loaded straight onto the railcars. In between the trestles is a structure made of a primitive concrete. This was probably a boiler room used to provide steam power for the continuous belts. There is supposed to be a brick building that was a power house and later converted to a box factory, but I did not locate it. Built of brick, it could still be standing and just missed by me in all the overgrowth. Numerous wells reportedly dot the area, but I did not spot any.

As mentioned before, the work was dangerous. Many men drowned or died from pneumonia. Some of their graves might be found at the nearby Fort Steele cemetery. The hacks also suffered from a condition called squeak heel. The constant exposure to cold water caused the contraction of muscles, in this case, the Achilles tendon. When this muscle tightened, the men ended up walking on tiptoe. It could take days to straighten out their legs correctly.

Access to the site is difficult. The easiest way would be by helicopter; if you don't own one, you'll have to walk in. One way is to cross the railroad bridge that sits between Fort Steele and the timber town. However, there are two problems: first, it is trespassing; second, it is dangerous. Long trains continuously cross this bridge, usually hauling Wyoming coal. The other way in is a dirt road near the I-80 Fort Steele rest area. The road isn't passable by vehicle because of the washed out bridges that cross numerous creeks and gullies. If attempting to hike, bring plenty of water and watch for rattlesnakes. Also, get written permission to access this land. L. M. Olson Company, which has a small gravel operation, owns the land. There is a locked and posted gate across the main road; a local man who lives in Fort Steele has the key to the gate. Walking through thick brush, I missed this gate. It wasn't until making follow-up phone calls that I found out about the land ownership and gravel operation. I had accidentally trespassed; to all those concerned, I sincerely apologize.

Much of the information for Carbon Timber Town and Fort Steele was obtained from park employees of the Fort Fred Steele State Historic Site. Carbon Timber Town can be partially viewed from the old fort grounds on the west bank of the North Plate River.

COPPERTON (Carbon)
SITE NOT VISITED

There is a place to pull over on the north side of State Highway 70, about twelve miles west of Battle Pass. There are signs here with history and old pictures of what used to be Copperton. The actual site is a couple of miles away on private property. The ghost towns of Rudefeha and Dillon are on this same forest service road. These settlements were part of the copper boom in the Sierra Madre Range. After the mining booms, Copperton became a sheep camp with a couple of saloons before evaporating into history.

Top: This is the original town site of Coyote Springs; it has also been used as a ranch. To date, it is vacant.

Bottom: This is the twentieth-century highway location of Coyote Springs. The gas station, repair shop, and restaurant businesses are closed here; some are now being used as residences.

COYOTE SPRINGS (Carbon)

I have not found much written about this old watering hole. It could have been a stagecoach stop or other type of way station because its water would have been a precious commodity in this area. It has definitely been a stop on the Lincoln Highway on a sporadic basis and is comprised of two slightly separated locations.

The first one you will probably notice is on present-day Highway 30. No sign announces it, and the name has been removed from most maps. This more modern portion was probably constructed in the late 1940s and consists of a gas station, garage, and café combination. Despite the presence of a half-dozen vehicles, this place was not open on any of my visits. The residence behind the business is occupied.

The older portion is a bit west of Highway 30 but is visible from the road on private property. The old Lincoln Highway bed is still discernible running right in front of it. The road itself runs parallel with Highway 30 and rejoins just north of Coyote Springs. The structures here are an abandoned ranch and three other buildings. Two are from 1922 and one from 1935. The only other remains are old utility poles.

Above: These are some of the actual springs that lured the people here.

Left: This is a portion of the original Lincoln Highway.

This is a high-altitude desert plateau with a harsh environment. The summers are hot, the winters are cold, and the prairie is full of sagebrush and rattlesnakes. The springs attract birds from miles around.

CROSBY (Hot Springs)
SITE NOT VISITED

The remains of Crosby are located on County Road 433 outside Kirby and south of the sister ghost of Gebo. Dad Jones, a miner and prospector, started Crosby. In the 1890s, mining started in "Coal Draw" to supply coal for use in Thermopolis.

This was the birth of Crosby. It must have grown to a fair size for, in 1925, the school held 125 students. The mines closed in Crosby in 1932, and residents moved almost overnight.

Today, there is a diner, a house, one mine structure, and tailings for remains. It is hot in the summer and cold in the winter. The best time to visit is fall. Crosby is not listed on any highway maps to my knowledge but can be located on a state road atlas. A major oil field is now located just west of the Crosby site.

CUMBERLAND (Lincoln)
SITE NOT VISITED

This was a coal-mining town of two mines, the Cumberland #1 and #2. It is thought that it was named for an English county. All that's left are some foundations, tailings piles, and a badly neglected cemetery on the west side of State Highway 189 south of Kemmerer.

DILLON (Carbon)
SITE NOT VISITED

The town of Dillon was started overnight when the city's fathers of nearby Rudefeha decided one day in 1901 to close the town's saloons. Rudefeha was a company town, and company owners controlled the town. By the end of the next day, the saloon owners and some other merchants had moved one mile west and started a town that would serve all the desires of the local miners. Malachi W.

Dillon led this merry little band of businessmen. Dillon was a former soldier who had served under General George Crook. His business was a combination brothel, gambling establishment, restaurant, and saloon. Meals were free for those who drank at the bar. Some of the miners built log cabins here to be closer to the bars.

Dillon was known as a town of drinkers and troublemakers. When the mines folded in Rudefeha in 1907, Dillon died a slow death. Businesses declined further when a fire in 1915 destroyed the hotel and last store in town. The last saloon closed in 1917, signifying the end.

The old town site is located on Forest Road 862 a couple of miles north of the Copperton Junction. This is the heart of the Medicine Bow Mountains and National Forest. The scenery is fantastic and makes a great setting for hikers and photographers. The road is reported to be rough and the remains few. The Forest Service map shows the forest service road running through the center of the location. For some years, the first thing one noticed on approaching this site were twenty-foot wooden stacks. Upon closer examination, these turn out to be winter outhouses. This says something about the depth of winter snow in the area and the living conditions that boomers dealt with in this environment.

DINES (Sweetwater)
SITE NOT VISITED

This was a coal-mining town that ceased circa 1910. At one point, it was surrounded by three active mines, had a post office, and fielded its own baseball team. Dines is located about six miles northeast of Reliance. Take the Winton Road north until you reach Road 18, aka the Superior Cutoff, and then head west. The road will split almost immediately. Take the right fork. Much of the route is four-wheel drive and should be taken with caution. The environment is that of a high-altitude desert. Remains reportedly consist mainly of rubble, foundations, and abandoned rail lines. Winton, another coal-mining ghost, is located about three miles north of here.

DUNCAN, THE (Fremont)
SITE NOT VISITED

The Duncan is one of seven ghost towns inside the elbow formed by highways U.S. 287 and Wyoming 28. Five of these, including The Duncan, were mining towns. To be more precise, The Duncan was a gold mine and mining camp.

The first strike was made during 1911 and much development soon followed. An amalgamator and stamp mill were installed. Power was provided by steam. After three years of digging and fifteen hundred feet of tunnel, The Duncan closed in 1914 because of financial trouble.

In 1946, new owners pumped a lot of money and new equipment into the operation. They installed a new ball mill, a classifier, a concentrator, several agitator tanks, and eight flotation cells. After a year, they had processed just twelve tons of ore and obtained just $2,000 worth of gold—hardly a paying proposition but a common one in mining in the West.

During 1956, the mine experienced another spurt of activity. By this time, the mine was running on electric power instead of steam. A mile from here is the dormant Mary Ellen Mine. Atlantic City is located a couple of miles to the northwest. A topographical map is needed to find this old mine camp.

Reportedly, a good gravel road winds over Mill Hill and takes you southeast to The Duncan. The mine camp is built on top of a hill. Significant intact remains were standing in the 1970s. Buildings included a two-story dormitory, the mine head, a mill, repair shops, a small store, numerous sheds, several dozen homes, and other mine structures. Construction was of wood with tin roofs. The present condition is unknown to me. This place is not currently listed on Wyoming websites.

The environment is high-altitude desert, with plenty of sagebrush and rattlesnakes but no shade. The best time to visit is in the summer or early fall.

DUNN (Sweetwater)
SITE NOT VISITED

Dunn was a town of Chinese immigrants. Its peak population is reported to have been around two hundred. The men worked in the coal mines at nearby Rock Springs until the people of Rock Springs burned down the town of Dunn. It was an all-too-common problem that fear of racially different, cheap immigrant labor brought out the worst in many.

Remains are reportedly here but on a four-wheel-drive road. Winter is very harsh, and any rain can turn the road to Dunn into twenty miles of mud or, worse, a flash flood.

You can learn more about Dunn and the county by visiting the Sweetwater County Museum in Rock Springs, Wyoming.

EADSVILLE (Natrona)
SITE NOT VISITED

Eadsville was established as a mining camp in 1892. Within one short year, the population peaked at about five thousand people. The mines played out in a short time.

The site is south of Casper and located near the top of Casper Mountain at about eight thousand feet. The town and most of the mining were on the south side of the mountain in the Red Creek drainage area.

Reportedly, the only remains here are foundations, a dilapidated cabin, and a gravesite—not much for all the activity and people that were here. The route is a four-wheel-drive road. When it's not a drought year, the snow can be deep in winter. The best time to visit is from mid-June to late September.

Top: This Fort Steele structure was the powder magazine. It has also been used as a granary.

Bottom: This was once the Fort Steele home of Mr. Chatterton, who was the acting governor of Wyoming.

EAST PLANE (Sweetwater)
SITE NOT VISITED

Located just south of Reliance and at the end of Lionkol Road are the remains of the coal-mining town of East Plane. It was probably a company town. Lionkol Road is a very rough drive in good weather and not recommended in bad weather. East Plane is on private property and is also the site of an underground coal fire.

A few buildings from the post still stand, but in most cases, all that remain are chimneys.

FORT FRED STEELE STATE HISTORIC SITE (Carbon)

This location is included because it was a town at least once as part of its varied history. It began as a river crossing for both the Oregon Trail and Overland Stage Company. Many people drowned here, and some of them are buried in the Fort Steele cemetery. Eventually, the "Richards Toll Bridge" was built and was reportedly a very profitable operation. No remains exist of the bridge today. As the Continental Railroad pushed west, this was a natural place for the Union Pacific to cross the North Platte. Since Indians in the territory were extremely hostile to the encroachments, the U.S. government sent in troops in 1868. The land near the river crossing offered a natural site to set up an army post. Wood was close at hand for fuel and construction. Water was plentiful. The post was named for a Union Civil War hero, General Fred Steele. It was one of three Wyoming army posts constructed to protect the transcontinental railroad from Indian attacks. In 1879, a corrupt Indian agent named Nathan C. Meeker caused an uprising of the Indians in Northern Colorado. Troops from Fort Steele had to help suppress the hostilities.

The Army abandoned the fort in 1886, and then civilians moved into the establishment and used the vacant buildings as a supply station for local ranchers. After that, it became the headquarters of the Carbon Timber Company. In 1892, the Cosgriff brothers bought the place for $100. It then became a town with a hotel, granary, saloon, and more. A few years later, a fire destroyed most of the town. In 1903, the place was sold to the Leo Sheep Company and converted into a sheep station. The Union Pacific also built a caretaker's house next to its bridge over the North Platte. This building is still there today. After time, even the Leo Sheep Company left. The final blow came when I-80 missed this old Lincoln Highway stop by one mile, creating new Fort Steele, which is itself now a ghost. Today, Fort Steele is a State Historic Site and Park, and remains are scattered over the 137-acre park although many are merely foundations. The buildings that remain cover a span of at least sixty years including the few of the original Army post.

The bridge tender's house still stands although its foundation was being rebuilt on my visit. One book claims that this was the officers' quarters for the post, but a park supervisor told me this was not true. Most of the post's buildings are gone, yet the powder magazine still stands. It was built of stone and kept on as a granary. Holes at the top of the walls enabled airflow to keep the powder dry. There are at least a half-dozen other old army buildings, but in some cases, only chimneys still stand, pointing skyward bearing mute testimony to what once was.

An interesting building that overlooks the post from the southwest was once the home of Acting Wyoming Governor Chatterton. This structure was built or poured from an old type of concrete called grout and was made from burnt limestone and unwashed gravel. The walls are eighteen inches thick, and even the rafters and joists were poured.

The park has numerous plaques relating the history of the place and of various other buildings or remains. A tourist guide claims there is a visitor's center at this park, but it was not evident on my visit in 2002.

Top: The bridge tender's house, seen here, is having its foundation rebuilt.

Middle: This water pumping station drew water from the North Platte River for local municipalities.

Bottom: These were some of the newer structures in sight. They even had window air conditioners.

Fort Fred Steele Historic Site is one mile north of I-80 at exit #228. There is no shade or services. Across the North Platte from the fort lays the ghost of Carbon Timber Town.

FORT STEELE (Carbon)

As soon as you pull into town (and that's using the term "town" rather loosely), you'll see a sign proclaiming the place "Old Fort Steele." The sign is wrong. This is actually New Fort Steele, but it's a minor point, as neither really exists as a community anymore. Fort Steele was a highway interchange service town. To be more precise, it is Interchange #228 on I-80. There are a few buildings on both sides of the interstate.

The name, of course, was borrowed from a more famous neighbor one mile to the north, Fort Fred Steele State Historic Site. It appears that the combination of highway business and amateur historians was not enough to sustain the economic viability of this location. The south side consists of a composite gas station/store/garage business. At one time, this building was a Stuckey's. There is a sign on the front window stating, "Land for Sale." However, I did not determine if this was for the one building or the whole town. There

This abandoned gas station/restaurant was for sale on my last visit.

This building served as service center for a KOA campground.

is a second brick building that served as a mobile home court's office, laundromat, and store. Lastly, there is a vacant mobile home and some sheds. The construction appears to be from the late 1960s through early 1970s.

On the north side are a small number of homes, some vacant. Upon closer examination, one of the vacant houses showed signs of once being a business. This location hadn't been used as a commercial enterprise for some time, but the large external water storage tank was still standing in the backyard. Serving as the office and store for a KOA campground for a short while, the structure later became a mobile home court. After that, it was used as a home. Now it is vacant. There is one old building on the north side that is probably from the late 1800s; it served as the Catholic church for Hanna, Wyoming. During the mid-1980s, a gentleman moved it here with the intention of converting it into a Catholic shrine. When his project ran short of funds, he had to give up the ghost. He moved back to Denver and has since passed away. The church did not have a steeple, but a cut in the front of the roof shows where a cross used to be. At the time of my visit, the building was being rehabilitated. By whom and for what purpose, I could not find out.

This is an arid environment that is hot during the summer. It is best to carry extra water with you while you check out the area's ghosts, which include Fort Fred Steele, Carbon Timber Town, and Walcott. The road on the north side of town takes you directly to the remains of the old fort.

GEBO (Hot Springs)
SITE NOT VISITED

Gebo was a coal-mining town and probably started in the 1890s. Just south is the sister ghost of Crosby. Coal was sent from these locations to the town of Thermopolis. Its final destination was mostly the boilers of steam locomotives.

Old black-and-white photos show that this town was large and fairly well developed with a women's marching band and a school. Still, a number of homes were simple dugouts with rocks stacked around for walls. Other more substantial buildings were constructed of local rocks and mortar. Examples of both housing types can still be seen today.

Lumber was brought in from the mountains for additional building material and for support beams for the coal mines. Numerous mineshafts are still visible. Timbered entrances to these mines dot the area. This is a danger. Timbers rot, not only causing the mine to be unsafe but also leading to surface cave-ins. Coal mines are dangerous enough for professional miners; entering abandoned coal mines probably ranks up there with playing Russian roulette.

On maps, the roads to Gebo look like an easy drive, but websites say it requires a four-wheel-drive vehicle. One thing you can be sure of, there is no shade. To get to Gebo, go to Kirby and head west on Sand Draw Road then left on Gebo Road. The environment is harsh. The summers blaze from no shade and the rocks reflecting back the heat. Winters are cold and windy.

Besides the dilapidated housing and mines, other remains include a large blower or air pump to provide air for the miners, a few company buildings, and a couple of cemeteries. These graveyards are said to be mostly full of infants and children. This is common. The infant mortality rate was once much higher in this country and was accepted as a fact of life. The harsh environment of the Old West did not improve this situation. Examinations of graveyards often give an insight to local history. All too often, the graveyards of western mining towns reveal epidemics and mine disasters.

One important note: According to one source, citizens of Worland use this place for target practice.

GILLESPIE PLACE/RADIUM HOT SPRINGS (Fremont)
SITE NOT VISITED

This was an attempt by a woman and her daughters to start a health spa. I haven't confirmed it, but I believe their last name was Gillespie. They built the spa next to Radium Hot Springs. They touted the spring and its radium as a cure-all for a number of ailments. This was, of course, before anyone knew of radiation poisoning. I have not confirmed if there is actually dissolved radium in the spring, but it is possible. The spring empties toward nearby Strawberry Creek.

Also nearby are the remains of Lewiston. Just west of these two locations is Willie's Handcart site. This is a rest area, campground, and historical site maintained by the Mormon Church. The handcart site commemorates a group of Mormon emigrants led by Captain James C. Willie. Because of a lack of funds, this group pulled handcarts instead of using a team and wagons. It didn't work. Deep snow from an early winter and a lack of food and proper clothing forced the group to stop here and reorganize at the end of October 1856. They were rescued, but not before 77 out of 404 died. The survivors arrived at the Salt Lake settlement on November 9, 1856.

This area was the route for the Oregon Trail as well as the Mormon Trail. The place is remote but heavily visited because of the Mormon camp. Websites say this is a two-wheel-drive road, but topographic maps give the impression of a much rougher drive. The best time to visit is late spring or early summer. Rain can turn dirt roads into mud troughs and dry stream beds into raging torrents. Remains consist mainly of guest cabins from the health spa.

GUNN (Sweetwater)
SITE NOT VISITED

This was a coal-mining town from the 1920s and 1930s. Busy in its day, it is now mostly foundations and sagebrush. An archeological dig was conducted here, and as such, federal law protects the location. The archeologists concentrated on garbage dumps from the miners' households. The road to Gunn is rough and unmarked, and the site is on private property.

HARTVILLE (Platte)

This is an out-of-the-way, sleepy business ghost of a town. Hartville was a service town for the neighboring mining town of Sunrise. When the Sunrise mine closed in June 1980, Hartville lost most of its business and its reason for being. Mining may have been the downfall of this community, but it's not why the area was originally settled. The first commercial activities here consisted of saloons serving troops out of Fort Laramie and a stagecoach stop established by the late 1870s. Hartville claims to be the oldest continuously occupied town in Wyoming and to have the oldest operating bar in the state. This establishment even hangs a sign with this claim above its front door. Hartville also claims to have the oldest standing, though not operating, jail in the state.

The town peaked during Sunrise's mining days. During that time, Hartville had three churches, a school, a bakery, two grocers, numerous saloons, a dentist's office, a doctor's office, a small hospital, an opera house with apartments on the second floor, a railroad station, a firehouse, a jail, and more. A railroad spur ran from the mine at Sunrise to the trunk line at Hartville. The trunk line was the Colorado and Wyoming Railroad; it connected to a main east–west line of the Burlington Railroad.

During the town's heyday, housing was hard to come by. Neighboring Sunrise was a company town and thus had company housing. Still, there was a large demand for additional housing in Hartville for the service sector workers, railroad employees, and any overflow of miners from Sunrise. I do not know the number of workers employed at the peak, but when the mines closed in June 1980, the Sunrise Mining Corp. laid off 289 employees. Hartville has been shrinking ever since.

Today, there are three churches in town but only one still has services. There is a post office and two bars, including the one that proudly proclaims being the state's oldest. A few businesses have been converted into housing; many are just vacant. You will notice a fair amount of stonework around town, mostly attributed to one German family. The old stone jail still stands, but I don't know if this was their handiwork.

One kindly seventy-year-old gentleman by the name of Jesus J. Rodriguez gave me a tour of Hartville and neighboring Sunrise. Rodriguez had been born in Hartville and worked at the Sunrise mine from age eighteen until it closed—a span of twenty-seven years. As we toured, he pointed to various buildings or lots and explained

Top: A saloon and a gentlemen's club are among the variety of businesses that have occupied this building. Its last use was as a private residence.

Bottom: At one time, this building housed a bakery on the first floor and a gentlemen's club on the second. During my visit, it was being used as a residence. The false-front building next to it was a general merchandise store.

Left: The main business street in Hartville. The building at the extreme left in the photo claims to be the oldest bar in Wyoming and was still open for business on my visit.

This building is claimed to be the oldest standing jail in Wyoming.

the different enterprises that were conducted there. Very often, the term "cathouse" came up. Obviously, he was not referring to single animal pet stores. It was a little surprising just how many of these establishments once operated here. These and saloons formed a good portion of the business community. Interestingly, the town's three churches were just around the corner from this entertainment district, which really was Main Street.

Hartville is located five miles north of Guernsey on State Route 270 and is marked on the state highway map. Population is listed at seventy-six. The environment is semi-arid yet scenic. Advisement: There is very little in the way of services along most of Route 270.

HEART MOUNTAIN RELOCATION CAMP (Park)

This ghost was not a town; instead, it was a World War II Japanese American internment camp. After Pearl Harbor, Democratic President Franklin D. Roosevelt ordered all persons of Japanese descent who lived in Hawaii or on the West Coast to be rounded up and moved to camps in the country's interiors. Most of these sites were like Heart Mountain and quite remote. The majority of internees arrived in a railroad freight car.

The camp got its name from a nearby mountain. At over 8,100 feet, the peak is easily visible from the site. On my visit in late June, it

Heart Mountain City would have been a difficult place in which to plant a victory garden during World War II.

was still snow-capped. I find the name ironic and poignant, for one can be sure that many a heart was broken by the forced relocation. More than ten thousand Japanese and Japanese Americans were "relocated" here. Heart Mountain was Wyoming's third largest city during World War II, with a hospital, churches, a fire station, a high school, a laundromat, a movie theater, rows of barracks, and more. At first, the internees were treated as spies and traitors, but eventually they were allowed to work in local farm fields for wages. There was a severe farm labor shortage, and as the camps were located in rural areas, the solution was natural. The internees could spend their wages at the camp store or in nearby Cody if they were issued a pass.

The military designed, built, and ran the camps. Internees were housed in barracks, and the camps were laid out in the same manner as a small Army base. They also had high barbed-wire fences and guard towers, just like POW camps, which, in many ways, they really were. A small guard and staff contingent oversaw the camp and lived here also. At the end of World War II, all residents quickly left Heart Mountain Camp, and the place was abandoned.

Of the large number of these incinerators at the camp, this is the last one standing.

Top: This was a guard shack.

Bottom: Once numerous rows of these barracks stretched out over the sagebrush.

Right: This is the sole remaining structure still standing at Hecla, but it is surrounded by other foundations.

There are twice as many buildings here than the websites report: there are four instead of two. The building and sign from the original memorial are now gone; all that is left are some sidewalks, concrete, and a rock wall. A new plaque was placed here in 1977. As for the camp itself, there are two barracks, what appears to be an incinerator building, an administrative office, sidewalks, concrete slab foundations, an abundance of utility poles, and debris. There are small wooden stands of the type used by the Army to lead exercises. One can only guess what they were really used for. There is supposed to be a cemetery here, but I didn't locate it.

This place is situated on the west side of Highway Alt 14 between Cody and Ralston. A large stone sign on the highway serves as a marker.

HECLA (Laramie)

This site shows on numerous maps and highway atlases but has little in the way of remains. Hecla was a small mining town during the late 1800s. There were three mines named Hecla, and the community took its name from them. It is thought they mined silver, but this is not confirmed. Boomers tried to attract the railroads, but the Union Pacific chose to run their line farther south. The mines weren't highly

productive, and investors couldn't be found. After a short while, the miners and their families packed up and left.

Later, this site became a town servicing the local ranchers. There was also a school. Both the new town and school took the old name Hecla. The town died again during the late 1940s, but the school carried on into the 1950s. There are no remains of the second town or its school. From the first Hecla, there is one mine, a building, and the foundations of two additional structures. The construction is of sandstone and timber. One large, three-tiered foundation appears substantial enough that it might have been a stamp mill or smelter. All remains are on posted private property but are viewable from a public road. There are some houses in the area, built after the second Hecla.

The environment is semi-arid, the topography rugged, and the scenery beautiful. Just to the west is Vedauwoo Rocks. Hecla is located on the north side of County Road 210, aka Crystal Lake Road. It may be reached from I-80 via exit #335 and the Buford Road in the south or State Highway in the north. County Road 210 is an all-weather gravel road. The area can be snowed-in during winter. The best time to visit is late spring through early fall.

The foundation in the foreground is of a modern type and may have been the school. The foundation in the background is made of stone and is from the town's mining period.

INYAN KARA (Crook)

This is a mixed site that I stumbled upon on a pass-through. The area is bisected by State Highway 585 and is near the midpoint between Sundance and Four Corners at the western edge of the Black Hills. This was a scattered farming and ranching community, and as such, the remains are also widely scattered throughout the valley.

As you approach from the north, a historical marker is on the west side of the road. This marker commemorates one of the first country churches in Wyoming and maybe the first permanent one in the valley. Reverend D. B. Chassell and citizens of the Inyan Kara community built the Inyan Kara Methodist Episcopal Church in

1891. The old church site is one mile west of the marker. A look through the binoculars showed no remains on the distant horizon.

A few miles south, on the east side of State Highway 585, is the Inyan Kara cemetery and a single abandoned building, which appears to be a one-room schoolhouse but could be the old Inyan Kara church. Although it has no steeple or any other religious fixtures, it does resemble the building etched into the aforementioned historical marker and could have been moved to this spot. The building is of clapboard construction with a stovepipe protruding from the center of its small roof.

Farther south on this highway and on the other side of the road is a boarded-up twentieth-century farming residence. Over a half-dozen old frame or log structures surround this house. It is obvious that these buildings were constructed at a much earlier date than was the central house. Immediately behind this group are an additional four or five collapsed log structures. The place gives the impression

Here are mixed remains of a ranch and town site combined.

Above: This was probably a smokehouse.

Left: The roofs and lumber used in these adjacent buildings illustrate two periods of construction.

as having been more than just a collection of ranch sheds. There is one more standing log structure about two hundred yards north of these buildings. All are vacant. The shadow of an old roadbed runs through the location and heads west; this was the old trail that leads to Inyan Kara Mountain. This was the actual old town site of Inyan Kara itself, and it is easy to see that the place has been reoccupied several times—not as a town but as a ranch and farm. Other abandoned farms and ranches dot the landscape of the valley.

Most of these buildings appear to have been built at the same time as well as vacated at a mutual time, at two different time periods. That is, you'll see structures made of logs all in the same stage of decay. Then there are newer buildings of modern construction with peeling paint. It is as if the valley was settled twice and abandoned twice.

The name's origin is Native American but over time has been misinterpreted, mispronounced, and misspelled by white settlers. An adjoining creek and a mountain that overlooks the area bear the same name. The word Inyan means "stone" in the Dakota Sioux language, but the meaning of Kara has been lost in time. It's most likely a corruption of some other word or words. Some claim it was the word Kaga, meaning "to make," "to cause," or "to form." It is further said the Sioux called the mountain Inyan Kaga Paha; Paha means "peak." This would make the name "stone made peak." For a mountain of broken volcanic rock, this makes sense.

The Inyan Kara Methodist Church is located a few miles north of the town site. This is the second location for the church. The first one is out on the prairie, a few miles to the northwest.

This same location was probably also the site of Camp Bradley, the fourth base camp of Professor Walter P. Jenney's 1875 expedition. This was a government expedition sanctioned by the Department of the Interior to assess the potential for land development in the Black Hills. The land had not yet been purchased from the Indians, but the department was confident the matter would be resolved to the government's liking.

General Custer also traversed the valley during his 1874 Black Hills expedition. These weren't the first two white expeditions to the Black Hills—they weren't even the first two expeditions to Inyan Kara—but they were probably the most important. The Custer party climbed the summit and while there allegedly chiseled "74 Custer" in the rock. Some say it is still there as a ghostly reminder of our not-too-distant past. There is some controversy over exactly what was carved, as sources disagree. One source says the rock carving stated "GAC US 7th." A photo in one book shows "G.C. U.S. 7," but the photo is uncaptioned and Custer was known to leave his carved initials over a number of locations in the Hills. A magazine article from 1971 states that these initials have disappeared. The Forest Service was unusually vague and unhelpful to my queries about the carving because of their concerns over protecting such historic sites from the constant scourge of vandalism.

This is a place of wind and waves of gently swaying grass. It makes you feel that, if you were to listen carefully, you could almost hear the faint call of a bugle just over the next ridge melodically playing "Gary Owen."

JAY EM (Goshen)

Jay Em is an early twentieth-century agricultural town that grew up before the Depression. Farmers had moved in to homestead land that had yet to be settled, and Jay Em was established to service the new local farmers. The town consisted of simple buildings made of mostly local materials. These were all businesses that serviced the local area at the time. There was no church, school, community

Top: This is a 1920s-era service station.

Bottom: Still completely intact, this was a very large lumberyard.

center, municipal organization, or city government. Lake Harris, who filed a homestead claim in 1912, started the town. Jay Em got its name from the initials of local land and ranch owner Jim Moore.

Today, this is a business ghost. There is a small population, and most are lifelong residents. The town is predominantly a concentrated one-square-block business district, with all buildings within a block of one another. There was a bank, repair shop, gas station,

The whole place has the appearance of an outdoor museum, down to the historical signs in the windows.

general store, hardware store, lumberyard, post office, stone cutting operation, and water tower. Jay Em streets weren't paved, and amenities such as curbs and sidewalks outside the business district were ignored.

The 1930s brought the Dust Bowl and the Great Depression. Strangely enough, improved roads and the increased use of automobiles led to further decline. Ranchers and farmers now drove greater distances to bigger towns such as Lusk to conduct their business. Soon the businessmen closed their shops and moved to where the business traffic was located. Most were gone by the late 1950s.

The old business district is quite a gem. Most of these concerns appear as if they are still open for commerce. Their interiors are in excellent condition down to pencils and ledgers on the counters. Signs are posted on doors describing the business and its years of operation. The stone mason shop still has small boulders in its workyard waiting to be cut. Sidewalks appear in both concrete and wood in the business section. The whole place resembles a large outdoor museum. Across the creek from most of the town are a cemetery and an abandoned city park. Many of the stones in the cemetery were cut and inscribed at the town's stone mason shop. There are a few additional vacant mercantile establishments and residences along the highway at the turnoff to Jay Em.

Jay Em is easy to find; it appears on the official state highway map. There isn't a highway sign to announce the approach, but there's a rather dated, handpainted, weather-beaten, metal pole with a plastic sign that marks the spot. The town is twenty-three miles south of Lusk on State Highway 85. There is no shade or services on this highway. At the Fort Laramie Road, head west. The town is just yards down the road. Rawhide Creek flows next to the site with JM Creek joining in just above the town. Currently, there is a church and a post office here, but no other services are available. Elevation is 4,615 feet.

JEFFREY CITY (Fremont)

One of the best ghost towns in Wyoming—or anywhere for that matter—but disappearing fast, Jeffrey City is one of Wyoming's twentieth-century uranium-mining ghost towns. This town started in the late 1800s as a pony express and stage station stop.

In 1982, this street was lined with brick homes. When I stared down this street, in my mind I could still hear the sounds of children playing and cars pulling in the driveway with dad coming home from work.

Most of it was built as a company town in the 1950s, a full-service community for the employees and families of a nearby uranium mine. This was dictated by the lack of significant housing or services for at least sixty miles. Housing styles were mixed, but all were modern designs. There were ranch-style houses, duplexes, two-story townhouse apartments, and barracks-style quarters for bachelors.

The town had three fire departments, a K–12 school with gymnasium, a community center, tennis courts, service stations, churches, a tavern, a liquor store, a bowling alley, a post office, and more. Today, only the post office and a Catholic mission are open. Whole blocks of housing have been removed from their concrete slab foundations and taken to places unknown. The streets are paved and, even where the housing is gone, lined with utility poles, street

lamps, signs, and fire hydrants. The signs bear names such as Sage Brush Lane and Jack Pot Drive. On my last visit, I spotted more antelopes than residents. There are a little more than fifty people calling this place home. At its peak, the population is estimated to have been at least six thousand.

The ore mined from here was processed into nuclear weapons during the cold war. When the cold war ended, Jeffrey City lost its economic base. The mines were closed during the early 1980s. By this time, the United States was committed by treaty to maintaining fewer nuclear warheads than it already had. This and the atomic energy industry's decline led to no market for Wyoming uranium.

On my last visit, there were over thirty vacant buildings, and that was only half of what I had seen five years earlier. This place is disappearing fast, yet it's just now starting to appear on websites.

Above: If you couldn't buy it here, it was a long way to the neighboring towns of Landers or Rawlins.

Top left: Although Jeffrey City had several service stations at its peak, only one was still open on my last visit.

Bottom left: Jeffrey City had a couple of houses of worship. This is the last one to hold any services. It continues to operate on a part-time basis.

Top: Many apartment buildings still stand here while the majority of the homes and duplexes have been torn down.

Middle: This was a bachelor's quarters. Most of the housing was divided between families and single men.

Bottom: Jeffrey City's numerous services are all closed now.

Jeffrey City is a ghost with sidewalks and telephone booths! Tennis courts have grass growing through the cracking concrete. The people that do live here generally live in their own mobile homes instead of the company housing that was left behind. Residents also have the benefit of the gymnasium, which has remained open. This is a very large, modern, multimillion-dollar building that wasn't even completed until the 1980s. The school had completely closed down, but recently the elementary section has reopened with nine students in attendance. At one time, part of the school was used as a game warden's house according to a conversation I had in 2002 with the workmen performing building maintenance on the school.

Older children attend school in Lander. Contrary to website reports, the post office is still open. Also open for business is St. Brendan's Catholic Church, a rather small house of worship constructed of steel and aluminum siding. Websites refer to a youth hostel and old mission run by a Father Rodriguez. These two places may be one and the same, but this is only conjecture. I just did not see anything else occupied. This is a true ghost. You look down the street and expect to see children playing, but instead only the occasional tumbleweed greets you.

Jeffrey City is located on Highway 287 adjacent to the old route of the Oregon Trail. Most of the town is on the south side. Lander is sixty miles to the west, and Muddy Gap is twenty-three miles to the east.

JELM (Albany)
SITE NOT VISITED

This was a logging town for the Union Pacific Railroad. Timber was in great demand for use as railroad ties for a branch line running south off the transcontinental railroad. This branch line served mining towns in the southeast section of the Medicine Bow Mountains before continuing south to additional mining towns in Colorado. Jelm was established along with Albany, Foxpark, and Woods Landing in the early 1880s. The rail line did not pass

New structures mix with old ones all over Keystone.

through Jelm; it lay about a half-dozen miles to the west. This was not the best route south into Colorado, but it was selected because it was closer to the mining towns it was built to serve. The area was stripped of timber by the early 1890s, and Jelm lost its reason for being. The rail line has since been abandoned, and the tracks have been taken up.

The DeLorme atlas of Wyoming shows the location of New Jelm on State Highway 10. The original location of the old Jelm town site lays roughly to the east of here on Jelm Mountain. The site is on private property, and permission must be obtained to visit it. Remains are said to be two cabins and a combination church-and-school building. The ages of the remains are unknown. For instance, the church might have been built late in the town's history. Old West lumber camps rarely had a church or school.

The information for this location was obtained from maps and by interviewing residents of Woods Landing.

KEYSTONE (Albany)

Keystone is located in the heart of the Medicine Bow Mountains and National Forest. Founded in 1878 as a gold-mining boomtown, it was first called Douglas Creek. It started with panning and moved on to large-scale dredging on Douglas Creek along with a number of hard-rock mineshafts. The first mine of Albany County, the Morning Star on the west bank of Douglas Creek, operated nearby. The Keystone mine sits on the east bank of Douglas Creek; it is marked on maps and is easy to find. Located in the center of town, the runoff of mine waste makes it easy to spot. Douglas Creek is still scarred today with large piles of gravel from heavy dredging and hydraulic mining techniques. The expanse of area this and other old mining operations cover might surprise you.

After the mining boom ended, timber workers moved in to log the area, and they made the town on Forest Road 542 their home. Douglas Creek flows next to the site, and the Bobbie Thomson National Forest campground is nearby. The scenic road to Keystone

from Albany is well marked and has abundant wildlife. Mine tailings and the old wagon road are still visible on this eastern approach. The other approach road is even more scenic but narrow. Snow could be a hazard, especially west of Keystone because of higher road elevation. In fact, I got stuck in a snowdrift on this road, and it took me three hours with an army entrenching tool to dig my way out. This part of the National Forest is called the Savage Wilderness Area.

The town itself, mostly a summer cottage community, is a blend of old and new construction. Some of the cottages are modern while others are just updated log cabins. A fair number of boom period buildings are used as sheds, and still others lay about in various stages of collapse. On the north side of town is a staged structure constructed as a tourist photo opportunity. It is a set of false fronts with no buildings, just picnic tables in the rear.

In addition, there is the Keystone Work Center. Part of the Medicine Bow National Forest, it has not been used as a work center since the late 1980s. Instead, keeping in vogue with the rest of Keystone, the structures are rented out as summer cabins. Horse corrals

Top: These false fronts were constructed for tourists.

Below: At Keystone, Douglas Creek is choked for miles with gravel beds, caused by dredging operations that dug up the creek bed in the search for gold.

Its large size and numerous doors reveal that this building was probably a business establishment.

are included. The center is under a tree canopy and in excellent condition. Most of these structures probably date from the 1930s. Persons who wish to rent one of these facilities should contact the headquarters of the Medicine Bow National Forest to request a reservation.

Recently, Keystone has been disappearing from a number of maps. The only other remains of the boom era are all the piles of gravel waste in Douglas Creek. These are even visible from the Bobbie Thomson campground. I used this place for my evening stop and had an interesting wildlife experience.

Three elk (and elk come in only one size—extra large) decided to pass through my camp. At first I didn't know what was coming my way out of the brush and the dark. I started waving my arms and yelling. This panicked the elk, and they stampeded. They thrashed about the campground, and my campsite was in a state of wild confusion for the next two minutes. Large branches were ripped off trees and trash cans trampled. It took what seemed like an eternity for these manic behemoths to reunite and head out of the campground together.

Above: Small houses still line the streets of Bosler.

Right: This small cluster of cabins was once a railroad boomtown in Piedmont.

Left: This was the main business street in Jay Em. Notice the sidewalks were paved but the street wasn't.

Below: On your travels through Wyoming, altitude can be a factor.

WELCOME
SUMMIT REST AREA
HIGHEST POINT
ON INTERSTATE 80
ELEV 8640
WYO DEPARTMENT
OF TRANSPORTATION

Right: This Jeffrey City community center was completed in 1982 and closed almost immediately afterwards.

Below: Another scene in Bosler.

Above: This Medicine Bow building contained a post office on the left and a grocery store on the right. Only the post office was still in operation on my visit.

Left: Loss of highway traffic to the interstate hit the Rock River business district hard. Located near the railroad tracks, these two buildings are from the town's railroad boom days. The house on the right was once a hotel.

KIRWIN (Park)
SITE NOT VISITED

Gold was discovered at Kirwin in 1885, but a town was not immediately established. This is a rugged and remote location that required at least some development. The site is located on the side of a mountain at the nine-thousand-foot level. It took until 1894 before an enterprise by the name of the Shoshone River Mining Company was formed to mine this discovery. It wasn't until 1897 that the first gold ore was shipped out. There was no mill to process it here. The ore was transported either by wagon or mule train. By then, Kirwin had thirty-eight buildings, including a sawmill, a hotel, a post office, stores, boarding houses, and more than a score of residences. The population peaked at about two hundred at this time. Strangely, the town had no brothels, saloons, or cemetery. The complete absence of brothels and saloons often denotes a community as a company town.

Because of Kirwin's location, the place suffered the deprivations of elevation, isolation, and weather. Blinding blizzards would shut everything down for days. The people that lived here had to be especially hardy to endure winters at this elevation. Often, mountain towns, even gold-mining towns, shut down until the spring thaw but not here. In 1907, they paid the price for such a hazardous lifestyle.

For eight days and nights, Mother Nature buried the town under tons of snow. An avalanche raced down the mountain, crushing part of the town and killing three people. One can only imagine the terror of the townfolk trapped by the storm in their homes, listening to the thunder of the oncoming white death. They had to wait for the weather to clear before they were able to dig out survivors or bodies. Parts of the town were buried under anywhere from fifty to one hundred feet of snow and ice. Living here was not only tough but also expensive. Instead of rebuilding the town, they closed the mine. The victims of the avalanche were buried at the Meeteetse Cemetery.

Carl Dunrud bought the town site and much surrounding land in the 1930s and built a ranch named the Double D Dude. Among some of the first guests were Amelia Earhart and her husband, George Putnam. Reportedly, she fell in love with the place and had asked Dunrud to build her a cabin. She planned to return to the Double D Dude and relax after her flight around the world. However, in 1937, she failed in this attempt and disappeared forever with her navigator, Frederick Noonan. Construction of her cabin, which had only reached four logs high, was halted.

Kirwin is accessible only in summer, and even then a four-wheel-drive vehicle is required. It is claimed that many buildings remain and include a church, cabins, and work sheds. The years and denomination of the church are unknown to me. My sources do not mention a church at Kirwin during its peak years, but this does not preclude it either. The remains of Amelia Earhart's unfinished cabin can be seen by hiking past Kirwin down a trail for about one mile.

All remains are unconfirmed and their condition unknown by me. There is a public campground in the area on the Greybull River at the end of Forest Service Road 208 and two on Wood River on Forest Service Road 200. I could find neither Kirwin nor the Double D Dude Ranch nor any evidence of either on any maps or atlases. All information presented here about Kirwin came from websites. If hiking in the area of Kirwin, keep the high altitude and mountain weather in mind.

Kirwin is located west of State Highway 120 near Meeteetse, Wyoming. A website says that you take State Highway 290 from Meeteetse until you reach Sunshine and that Kirwin is a few miles west of there. I had a very difficult time locating the town of Sunshine. From its position on a highway atlas from the 1970s, it was south of the location described on the website. Using the atlas, you follow Highway 290 until you reach Wood River Road. Take a left onto Wood River Road and follow it approximately six miles. This should put you in the town of Sunshine; that is, if it is still there. Sunshine Creek and Reservoir is in between the larger V formed by Highway 290 and Wood River Road. Kirwin is supposed to be a few miles beyond this point. To locate this ghost, I suggest you ask locally. Directions might be obtained in Meeteetse.

LAVOYE (Natrona)
SITE NOT VISITED

Lavoye was named after homesteader Louis Lavoye and was reportedly short-lived. It was built as a bedroom community for the nearby Salt Creek Oil Field. The area is remote, even by Wyoming standards. There are no residents here. State Highway 259 will get you to the Salt Creek Oil Fields; after that, ask directions at Salt Creek Camp.

To travel off the highway, a four-wheel-drive vehicle would help. There is a historical marker on Highway 259, and the infamous Teapot Dome is just to the northeast. Remains are said to be numerous and substantial, but this is unconfirmed.

LEE CITY (Park)
SITE NOT VISITED

I found this location on only one website. The history of Lee City is sketchy. It was supposed to be a gold-mining town. Its name, as was common practice at the time, might have come from southern Civil War vets turned prospectors.

There are no residents, and remains are said to be three broken-down structures with, perhaps, more remains one mile farther up the trail. To get there, you go west on Highway 296 to Sunlight Road; turn here and drive to the first and only ranger station. Ask directions here; a map is recommended. The roads are four-wheel drive farther up the line and could be closed because of mud, snow (even in July), or grizzly bear habitat protection. Bear spray is a prudent precaution. You will probably have to hike to the sight and will be forced to ford a swift mountain stream.

LEWISTON (Fremont)
SITE NOT VISITED

This was a mining town founded along Strawberry Creek in 1879. Today, all that remains are two buildings and some foundations on private property. In 1861, the site had been a pony express station. The town of Lewiston mined gold, silver, and copper ore. There are many abandoned mineshafts in and around the town. Some are near the surface and in danger of collapse.

A lot of the mining activity consisted of a process called "salting." This is a scam whereby a person actually places gold, silver, or another ore somewhere and claims this is a genuine strike. The land is then sold to the first unlucky sucker the scam artist can lasso. What there were in the way of real mines were played out by the early 1890s. Some prospectors and their families hung on to the area until the 1970s.

At its peak, Lewiston was only about twenty-five buildings, four of which were saloons. Of the two structures that survive today, one was a general store owned by the Gusin family and the other was a livery building. The only other remains are debris, foundations, and the ruins of a mill a half mile away on Strawberry Creek.

MANVILLE (Niobrara)

Manville is one of many agricultural and railroad communities that are withering on the vine. Today, its population is listed as ninety-seven, but if you go there, it is easy to see that the total was once

Above: This is the Manville school. Despite being boarded up, the lawn is still mowed.

Left: This is the Manville store, a general merchandise establishment.

Top: The business district at Manville is a combination of small false-front buildings and two-story brick structures.

Bottom: The center of the oil town McFadden.

much higher. Empty streets, vacant lots, and isolated fire hydrants mark old boundaries that no longer matter.

The first railroad here was the Fremont, Elkhorn & Missouri Valley. Union Pacific Railroad later bought up this route. The UP line still runs through Manville but no longer stops here. Passenger service ceased soon after WWII, and the old depot has since been converted into a house. Freight and grain trains discontinued stopping here a couple of decades later.

The bank failures of the late 1920s, the Dust Bowl, and the Great Depression all hit Manville hard and hit her at her peak. Manville once had a lively dance hall that used to fill up on weekends. Then, new roadways were constructed south of Manville, taking increasingly more business traffic elsewhere. Most surviving local businesses have moved to Lusk, Wyoming. Van Tassel and Jay Em have suffered much the same fate although the latter never had a railroad.

Today, most business buildings here are either vacant or converted to another use. There is an out-of-use post office, and one old business building has a false front. The school is boarded up and vacant. There is a sawmill, but it too is silent these days. A few of the abandoned businesses are two-story brick structures. About half the homes, including some of the newer ones, are empty. Local services consist of a gas station on the highway, a new post office, and one open church. One note of interest: Many of the homes here have wooden shingle roofs.

Manville is located in eastern Wyoming, just north of the intersection of Highway 18 and State Route 270. Since the elevation here is 5,245 feet, almost a mile high, the air is a little thin. Also, since this is Wyoming, the place is windy. On my visit, there was a gentle breeze of forty miles an hour. This town is marked on the official state highway map and is easy to find. It has many unoccupied buildings and presents a good photo opportunity.

McFADDEN (Carbon)

McFadden is located on State Highway 13 in the center of Carbon County. This is a little used stretch of road. The town shows on all atlases and state highway maps. According to website reports, there are currently no residents at this site, making the place a recent ghost. Websites also state this was a service town for the ranch industry. Upon my arrival, I saw no evidence of such services—no old tractor dealership or gas stations; instead, this appears to have been a company town of the oil industry. Further research confirmed that this town was established by the Ohio Oil Company and named for the man who founded the company. While ranches surround McFadden, it is also in the middle of an oil field. There are numerous oil tanks, derricks, and similar equipment scattered about town. A small number of homes, maintenance sheds, and one office are now occupied. This current activity could be due to the spike in the market price of crude oil, over $41 a barrel and climbing at the time of my visit. A sign pronounced the oil field as private property and referred to the local wells as the Rock River Field. The wells are low-production operations called stripper wells. There are no services other than oil field services.

As an energy bonus, a windmill farm flanks the area. Hundreds of whirling giants dot the horizon—enough to confound even the Man of La Mancha. Most of the town rests on top of a gently sloping

Left: These tiny cabins were company housing.

Top: A number of these equipment sheds were scattered over the site.

Middle: Streets and sidewalks expose McFadden's past as a much larger town.

Bottom: This is a playground that was being used for vehicle storage.

Above: On my last visit to Medicine Bow, only one service station remained opened for business; at least four others were closed. When the interstate bypassed this town, it lost nearly all its highway traffic.

Right: At the Medicine Bow Hotel, you can get a room or a great cheeseburger or maybe even bump into "Hal."

valley. Rock Creek meanders along the bottom of the valley. There are additional buildings along the creek; some are vacant, but most belong to working ranches.

McFadden has a "company" look. Some of the houses are small row cabins. Most of the structures, whether homes or sheds, are of an identical type of frame construction. Sidewalks, a basketball court, a playground, and a radio tower all point a finger at company life. Foundations and vacant streets attest mutely to this place's past size. There is a memorial in town with an accompanying flagpole, but its plaque has been removed. It now stands as a silent sentinel.

MEDICINE BOW (Carbon)

This is a wonderful ghost of a town. It is easy to reach, with plenty of vacant buildings to photograph and a good restaurant to boot. Medicine Bow got its start as a collection point for railroad ties that had floated down the Medicine Bow River. During the early 1860s, Union Pacific and Central Pacific railroads were rushing headlong across the west from opposite directions in a contest to see who could lay the most tracks for the first transcontinental railroad. The Union Pacific got to Wyoming first and ran its track alongside the Medicine Bow River for two reasons.

First, steam locomotives use lots of water. The second reason was
the supply of railroad ties from the Medicine Bow Mountains.
Lumberjacks would chop down pines and cut them into railroad ties.
These men would roll the ties into the river and, using long poles,
would "herd" the ties downstream to a collection point with sorting
booms. They were paid at the end of each trip, giving Medicine Bow
another purpose. Soon, a couple of drinking establishments were set
up to give the lumbermen something to do with their money.

When the rail line was laid through here in 1868, Union Pacific set up
a railroad station and a water tank to service the locomotives. Slowly,
other buildings started to pop up, including a general store and a
saloon. The place soon became a shipping point for cattle and sheep
ranches. Settlers in this area came under frequent Indian attacks.
The town of Medicine Bow itself suffered at least two all-out attacks.
One kept the town under siege long enough for it to run out of food.
Cavalry from Fort Steele came to the rescue and saved Medicine Bow
as they did other towns.

During the 1870s, the government built and operated a commissary,
post office, and elementary school. J. L. Klinkenbeard owned the

The Medicine Bow Mu-
seum makes for a good
and informative stop.

general store. There was also a small hotel, a livery stable, and two small eating establishments.

The town got its name from the river running next to it. The river got its name from the mountains from which it flowed. The mountains got their name from the Plains Indians. It is thought the Indians named the area as they did because it was a good place to make bows and arrows, using the plentiful birch in the area.

Medicine Bow lays claim to fame through writer Owen Wister, who wrote the Western novel *The Virginian*. August Grimm built a hotel here, claiming it was in honor of Owen Wister, and named it the Virginian. I think he did it in honor of chasing profit. The town was still growing at this point. A book and a website say this hotel was built in 1913. I stopped and had lunch at the Virginian where I was given a pamphlet citing the history of the hotel and town. This document claims the hotel was built in 1909. A sign on the building claims 1905 as a building date. Whatever year it was built, it is a beautiful building. It is a three-story stone structure in excellent condition and still operates as a restaurant, saloon, and hotel. There are twenty-one rooms laid out in grand Old West style. The hotel was constructed with electric lights, indoor plumbing, and steam heat, and it has been kept up to modern standards while retaining its authentic Western charm. Its last major rebuild was in 1984.

Keeping in the spirit of things, the hotel is also allegedly haunted. The story is that a man came to the grand opening of the hotel where he was supposed to meet his lady love. She never showed, and he died of a broken heart at the hotel

Top: This is the old town square. Notice the numerous false fronts.

Middle: This is one of several closed grocery stores.

Bottom: This was Medicine Bow's bank. It is now a second-hand store but has not been open on any of my visits.

while waiting for her. Legend is, he never left. The waitress referred to him as "Ol' Hal."

You are allowed to wander around and tour the place while waiting for your meal. Unoccupied rooms are kept open for display. Owen Wister never saw the hotel, and I'm not sure that he had ever been in Medicine Bow. As he says in his book, he worked at a nearby ranch. Contrary to some reports, he did not go west to gather material for his book; he went for his health, which he did at the age of twenty-five. Wister spent nineteen years on the Wyoming frontier, and the life he experienced was the basis for his book. The book later became a movie and a television series.

Another building of interest is the "Dip Bar." Inside is a collection of intricate woodcarvings and a handpainted dance floor. The most striking thing though is the bar itself. It is forty feet long and carved from a single four-and-one-half-ton jade boulder. The rock was discovered in Wyoming—some sources say near Lander, others claim at Rock Springs. This is reportedly the largest jade bar in the world.

The town was incorporated in 1909, and its first mayor was August Grimm. The Medicine Bow bank, a fine brick structure with pillars, was built in 1911. Bought by local ranchers in 1919, it was renamed Stockman's State Bank. This structure is still there today and makes a fine photographic subject. It has housed other businesses, including a second-hand store. The Union Pacific Railroad relocated its route through Rock Creek to Medicine Bow in 1901. A depot was built here, but it burned down in 1913 and was replaced in the same year with the current one.

Top: The sign says this church is open twice monthly; appearances say otherwise.

Middle: This newer retail establishment was built long after Medicine Bow's boom days.

Bottom: Once a business building during Medicine Bow's boom days, this old structure is now a private residence. Its history can be found in the Medicine Bow Museum.

This motel was one of many businesses in town that closed when the interstate was built south of here.

It is now the Medicine Bow Museum, conveniently across Highway 30 from the Virginian Hotel. In perfect condition, the depot looks like it belongs on a model railroad set.

The town faded slowly. Early on, ties and timber stopped flowing down the river. All the mining booms in the mountains to the south of town stopped early in the 1900s. Then, when the interstate was built, it bypassed this section of Highway 30. Union Pacific stopped passenger rail traffic a long time ago, which explains why the railroad depot is a museum.

This is a semi-ghost. The population is listed as 274 on the state highway map. On my visit, the highway sign said 389. In my opinion, the lower of the two numbers, or an even lower figure, would be more accurate. Many homes are abandoned, but I recommend you don't tell local residents they live in a ghost town. That is not the way the residents view things. Please respect private property rights. You can't always tell which building or home is abandoned. There are numerous vacant businesses. Many have been modified or rebuilt multiple times. Still, it is easy to spot false fronts. Some buildings are from this town's frontier days. Others, such as the vacant motel, are newer. One of the town's grocery stores has a false front, constructed of cinder block. Parts of the livery stable stand but had been converted to other businesses since its original days.

Besides the Virginian Hotel and the gas station, the only other services I spotted were a church, a liquor store, a small motel, and the post office. There are many other abandoned buildings, including a large modern school and library, part of which is being used as a community center. A church, a fire department, a garage, a liquor store, a meat market, mobile homes, and much more sit silently. Some of the oldest part of town is on the south side of the tracks, but there's not much left. Still, its history is interesting to check out at the Medicine Bow Museum.

The Medicine Bow Elementary School is now vacant. The high school attached to it is now being used as a senior center.

Medicine Bow is located along the old Lincoln Highway 30. Lincoln Highway was conceived in 1912 and completed in 1913. The road was built quickly by linking existing dirt roads that ran along railroad right-of-ways. This was the first United States continental road route, but for great stretches, it is nothing more than a wagon road. The original route, free of railroad property, was completed in 1922. Paving the entire route wasn't finished until the 1930s. The first car in Medicine Bow beat the road by ten years. Dr. Horatio Nelson Jackson stopped here for gas in June 1903. August Grimm had heard of Dr. Jackson's endeavor and, being a good businessman, had arranged for five gallons of gas to be sent to Medicine Bow. Grimm then charged the good doctor $5.25 a gallon, a price that drew a terse mention in Jackson's travel journal.

Almost a hundred years later, on my first visit to Medicine Bow, I couldn't buy gas for any price. When I stopped here in 2004, there was an operating gas station, but four others were closed. Much of the Lincoln Highway's route in Wyoming follows the trail blazed by Dr. Jackson. Interstate 80 follows some of the same route but leaves whole sections such as Highway 30 to wither on the vine. There are two 1928 Lincoln Highway markers in town; one is in front of the museum, and the other is in front of the Virginian Hotel. Both the town and the hotel have their own websites. The hotel is also a national historic landmark. Union Pacific tracks are still in use, running along the southern edge of town.

The elevation is 6,565 feet. It can be windy, and winter can blow snowdrifts onto the highway of these high plains.

MILFORD/NORTH FORK (Fremont)
SITE NOT VISITED

In 1878, Ase Wilson built a mill on this site, which was founded around 1874–1875 as the community of North Fork. Wilson was said to be a cousin of General William Tecumseh Sherman and is buried in the Masonic cemetery north of town. In 1884, Milford, as the town was now called, was passed over for the county seat in favor of Lander. Its main source of economic activity appears to have been the soldiers from nearby Fort Washakie visiting the town's saloons and red-light district.

When the fort and mill closed, so did most of the town. At one time, there was a brick schoolhouse, several stores, saloons, a gentlemen's house, a main street, and a small number of well-built homes.

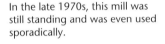

In the late 1970s, this mill was still standing and was even used sporadically.

This piece of equipment was probably simply too heavy to economically haul away from Mineral Hill.

Today, there is still a small population estimated to be about twenty residents. The community's two cemeteries are still here.

The Alton-Leseberg cemetery is located in Milford at the town's crossroad. The Wilcox-Masonic cemetery may be found one mile northeast of town on Second Street. It is claimed that Lena Canary Borner (sister of Calamity Jane) is buried in an unmarked grave in this cemetery.

Besides the cemeteries, the old millpond, a portion of a very dated saloon, the old main street in town, the Alton brick home, and the Nimple-Schwelder stone house remain here. Milford is located five miles north of Lander on Highway 287.

MINERAL HILL (Crook)

The information for this location came from one book and two websites. All three sources were word-for-word identical. The websites probably copied the book, whose information dates to 1974. Maps were the only additional source for information before my visit.

The dog's name was Rose, and, of course, she was from Texas. She joined me on the hike to Mineral Hill that day, and I even shared my lunch with her.

This was one of the workers' cabins. Numerous piles of lumber like this dot the area.

Mineral Hill was an on-and-off gold-mining operation, dating back to the 1880s. In 1904, there was a large twenty-stamp mill in the town of Welcome that processed the large amount of ore from Mineral Hill. This location is about one-half mile northwest of Welcome and two miles southwest of Tinton; it is bisected by Spotted Tail Creek. These are all remote locations situated within a maze of rough roads. All three are on posted private property, and locals discourage visitors. Winter or bad weather can make roads impassable. A topographic map and the ability to use it are required. The Forest Service owns the Mineral Hill fire tower on nearby Cement Ridge.

On my visit, I found mostly debris. Numerous old small dams across both Sand and Spotted Tail creeks are easy to see. One dam formed a small millpond that I had seen in an old black-and-white photo. Cattails now grow in the remnants of these ponds, and all the dams were breached. The impounded water would have been used for panning and ore separation. The mill was gone except for its concrete foundations and lots of lumber. Homes varied from dugouts to log cabins and newer structures. Even most of the older structures appear to have been wired for electricity although, in many cases, it was an obvious later addition. The only other remains were junked autos, equipment, and prospecting trenches.

Another major gold strike occurred nearby on Negro Hill. The Hill was named for the black miners who worked it. The gold ore from here was sent to the mill at Mineral Hill. There are no remains to my knowledge on Negro Hill.

At one time, Mineral Hill was a company town. Old photos show a number of intact structures. Construction was mostly rough lumber, so age has caught up with much of the place. The mill itself was said to be intact and operated on an irregular basis. The main mine, called the Prospect, is on the east side of the creek along with at least two others I found. The mine entrances are all collapsed.

Some sources claim that some or all of Mineral Hill is in South Dakota—this is not true; the entire site is in Wyoming. The road is very rough and shouldn't be attempted in bad weather. A tax assessment notice posted on a tree showed the area is still panned for gold. Many other metals, particularly tin, have been mined in the area, and remains of such endeavors can be found scattered about.

Best time to visit would be summer. The place is beautiful for hiking.

MINERS DELIGHT/HAMILTON CITY (Fremont)
SITE NOT VISITED

This is a gold-mining ghost that neighbors South Pass and Atlantic City. During 1867, a group led by Herman G. Nickerson discovered placer gold in Spring Gulch. They immediately laid out a town and named it Hamilton City. Soon, several mines were open in the area; the most productive was located on Peabody Hill and named Miners Delight.

Jonathan Pugh founded the mine during 1867–68. The vein here was rich, and the town soon changed its name to match that of its most productive gold producer. A ten-stamp mill was erected to crush the rock. The usual stampede of business followed. At first, stores were operated from tents along Spring Gulch. By the next spring, more substantial structures had been built.

The gold here was contained free in a vein of quartz. A mule-drawn arrastra crushed the quartz, and men panned out the gold. This was definitely a time for workers to do some "high grading." This mine closed down in 1874 but has reopened seven times since. Each time, the old shafts have to be pumped out of water and rebraced. The last time this mine was active was during the Depression. By that time, the operation had produced over $5 million in gold ore.

In the East, numerous places boast with a sign that "George Washington Slept Here." You see a lot of that out West; only the name is changed to "Calamity Jane." This is one of many South Dakota and Wyoming locations to lay claim to her fame or infamy.

Calamity Jane was born Martha Jane Canary. She was orphaned and adopted at a young age. Jane and her new parents moved to Miners Delight in 1867 or 1868. Here, Jane met a woman from the East. As the story goes, this woman talked Jane into a lot of things, including going to New York for a while. When she returned to Miners Delight, she went into the business of servicing miners. Later, she moved to Atlantic City and set up a dance hall. Next, she appeared in the Black Hills servicing the miners of another gold rush. Jane held a variety of jobs in her lifetime. One of these included passing herself off as a man to get a job as a wagon driver or teamster in the Black Hills during the 1870s. She gained notoriety here by making false claims about with whom she slept, like the infamous Wild Bill Hickok. Hollywood has done wonders reinventing this character of the past.

Today, the town is empty of mining activity and people. The land is owned by the BLM, and they have propped up the buildings. There is a nature trail and a fenced-in cemetery to go along with about a dozen buildings. These include a bakery moved from Fort Stambaugh and a church. This location is the old Fort Stambaugh Road about 3.5 miles from Atlantic City. A detailed local map would be good to have.

MONARCH (Sheridan)

This was a coal-mining town. Map searches show numerous abandoned coal mines in the immediate area. There is also at least one nearby mine that is still in operation.

Monarch is located off Interstate 90 northwest of Sheridan. It is on the west side of the highway by the exit for Acme. This location is on private property, and permission must be obtained from the Paddlock Ranch to gain access. A website claims you need written permission to take pictures. However, I interpret the law that if you are standing on a public road, you may legally take pictures of anything in public view. There are, of course, exceptions, such as military bases, photographing through windows, or taking pictures for marketing purposes. It's based on the legal principal of "an expectation of privacy." If your house is visible from the road, you can't expect people not to look at it from the road.

A coal-mining boom spawned a number of small towns. At the time, it was thought that the city of Sheridan would expand to here. In fact, a trolley used to run from Sheridan to these towns; the trip was only fifteen minutes. When cutbacks and lack of production caused most of the mines here to close, many of the families moved back to Sheridan and took their houses with them. If you drive around Sheridan, you can still find a number of these old homes.

Of the most significant remains is an old, beautiful church that has been converted into a residence. There are several other buildings, and one is reportedly now a meat store. There is a small population. Parts of the street grid still show here and on maps. This location is across the Tongue River, and a number of the original bridges are still present.

The communities of Acme and Kleenburn are on the opposite side of I-90. Both have a small population. There is an active coal mine nearby. Additional remains consist of two cemeteries, a bridge, some foundations, and an old power plant. The scenery is easily appreciated, and, if one is far enough off the interstate, it is quiet enough to hear the wind blowing through the sagebrush.

MOSKEE (Crook)

Sources conflict over this site's location and physical status. It clearly shows on all maps, including the official state highway map, situated directly on a county road. Still, one website claims it is four miles up a private drive instead. This source claims there is a single standing building, and the Homestake Mining Company has leveled the rest of the location. Another describes this location as a community of eight houses on Cold Springs Creek. There may be two locations with the same name, or this may be a mine or sawmill and the town that serviced the work site. Other books and websites claim there is much more to this location. Either the information is dated, or there were two locations.

I found Moskee simply by following the state highway map. The northern approach off I-90 down the Black Hills Grand Canyon is a very scenic route. Upon my arrival at Moskee, I noticed a sign stating that the southern approach was closed. The sign did not give a reason for the Forest Service road closure, and it did not say by whom or at what time it may reopen. Rather takes the meaning out of the word "service," doesn't it?

Moskee got its start in the early 1900s as a lumber and sawmill town. How and when the town got its present name is subject to conjecture. It was also known as (in probable order): Bearsville, Homestake Wyoming Camp, and Laviere. When the town applied for a post office in 1925, it did so under the name Laviere. It was rejected and resubmitted as Moskee. The Postal Department explained that the first name was too much like other Wyoming towns; Moskee was accepted.

Cut lumber was mostly milled into railroad ties by the McLaughlin Tie Company, which closed operations in 1907. A small cottage

This water tank was part of the town's firefighting system.

community continued here until 1921 when the Homestake Mining Company took over the area and developed the town extensively into a lumbering and sawmilling company town to provide timbers for its mine. Heavy trucks hauled out the logs, lumber, and mine timbers. Often, they used an old road built by the McLaughlin Tie Company during the early 1900s. Homestake built a sawmill, a large boardinghouse for loggers, a washhouse, a long maintenance building with boiler room and shops, at least a half-dozen houses, and a very large gravity-fed water tank. The tank got its water from a nearby spring and provided water for both the town and its fire hydrants, which had sheds over them to keep them free from snow during the winters.

Between the pine forest, frame buildings, and the sawmill, threat of fire was always a great fear.

The town grew slowly. The post office was added in 1925 and a school in 1928. At about this time, the company provided the town its own electric-generating plant. At its peak in the 1930s, there were about two hundred residents. During the Second World War, the mill and company town were closed and never reopened. After that, local hunters used the town on occasion.

When you arrive in Moskee, your first question will be, "Is this it?" You may then wonder why this place is on the state highway map. While this is beautiful country, there's not a town here. There is one house with "Moskee Wyoming" in raised metal letters on its front, but this is probably just a hunting cabin. Constructed of wood and still completely intact, the large water tank is still standing on the hill overlooking the town site, and its water flume lies strewn on the ground below. Three sheds that probably covered the town's fire hydrants also remain. In places, you see water valves at ground level with wooden boxes built around them. Other than these things, the only other remains are scattered debris, piping, or boards. Today, the area is still used for hunting and logging.

Top: This is a snow shed for a fire hydrant.

Bottom: This is the last intact building in the town of Moskee.

To reach Moskee from the north, take I-90 to exit #191 and then head south on Moskee Road for about twelve miles. This road runs through the town site. From the south, use Highway 85 and turn onto Forest Road 807 near the Hardy Ranger Station, which is a good place to ask for directions and to confirm that the southern approach is open. Check road and fire conditions or ask any other pertinent questions. Forest Road 807 ends as a "T" intersection at Road 207. Turn right, and Moskee should appear immediately.

Hams Fork Supply Company was once the most important business establishment in Opal. Now, its only purpose is to serve as a subject for photographs. During Opal's boom days, this business serviced local oil and railroad workers.

While Moskee is in the Black Hills, it is not within the boundaries of the National Forest. Remember, this is private property—treat it as such.

OLD UPTON/IRON TOWN (Weston)
SITE NOT VISITED

This is an artificial ghost town or tourist attraction. The location was originally called Iron Town, the name derived from nearby Iron Creek. This town was probably founded as a railroad town because of its water source. The Burlington Northern runs alongside. Later, the name was changed to Upton. Still later, Upton was moved a mile south. The reason and date are unknown to me. The current Upton has a population of 872 and is not a ghost.

The ghost is a mile north on the original Iron Town/Upton site. What you see here started in 1995 as an Upton High School project called "Old Town." Combining the names of the location and the project gave this place its name of Old Upton. This Old Town project collected and relocated buildings from ranches and ghost towns in Weston County. The structures date from the late 1800s to the early 1900s and were typical of

Wyoming from that period. Websites say this is on "County" Road 16 that runs from Newcastle to Moorcroft. The problem with this is that "U.S. Highway" 16 runs the described route, and County Road 16 doesn't appear on a Wyoming atlas. When I drove to Upton in 2000, I saw no sign of Old Upton.

These structures have been restored and include ranch buildings, homes, shacks, an old fire department hall, and Upton's first jail. The Black Hills abuts Thunder Basin National Grasslands here.

To be sure, ask for directions in New Upton. The residents are said to be very proud of their number one tourist attraction. The town fills up every third Saturday in July when it hosts an annual reunion for families and past residents. For more information, Upton even has a homepage.

OPAL (Lincoln)

Opal was founded as a Union Pacific Railroad town in the 1860s. Its location was chosen because of the availability of water in the Hams Fork River. These were the boom days for the railroad industry, and Opal boomed as a major shipping point. Major products shipped out were cattle, sheep, and wool.

Above: This historical marker is located next to the Hams Fork Supply Company.

Left: These structures are from Opal's oil boom period.

This town also experienced some activity because of the swings within the oil industry in Wyoming. Exploration was carried out in the 1860s through the 1870s and again in the 1920s, predominantly near the Hams Fork River. All the holes drilled turned out to be dusters. Some equipment remains are supposedly still visible in the area. Opal also served as a supply center for area ranchers.

Today, Opal is experiencing something of a rebound. A natural gas compressor station has been set up across the highway from the town. With the compressor plant comes employees. Many of these workers now have mobile homes in Opal. Some older structures were torn down, but the Hams Fork Supply Company building still stands. This two-story brick structure was a combination hotel, gas station, grocer, and liquor store. The liquor store portion had its own entrance. Next to this building is a stone monument dedicated to the Western pioneer. There is a railroad siding, but trains no longer make regular stops in Opal. There are a few abandoned homes and other structures from the railroad and oil boom days. Its population is listed as 102, but this seems optimistic. Its elevation is listed as 7,400 feet in books and on websites, but the official state highway map shows it as 6,668 feet. The town is situated on Highway 30 at the junction of State Highway 240.

The town gets its name from the semiprecious stones that litter the ground in great abundance here. The stones are common property and may be collected, that is, just as long as you are on public lands. Best time to visit would be late spring or early fall when the weather is at its best.

PACIFIC SPRINGS (Fremont)
SITE NOT VISITED

This spot was the first camping site for emigrants on the Oregon Trail after crossing South Pass. There were numerous springs that formed the headwaters of Pacific Creek. A town was founded in 1853 to serve the emigrants of the Oregon Trail and had a relay station for the Lander-Rawlins Stage Road. Later, stages and freight wagons from Point of Rocks passed through on their way to South Pass City. In its short history, the pony express relayed through here.

Pacific Springs is located southwest of South Pass on a swampy flat at 7,200 feet. Eight buildings have been moved away, but it is reported that five remain, including the town store and livery. The store was converted to a storage building for a ranch.

Initially selected for its water (springs), the location became known for its mud. Wagon trains camped a mile south of town on higher ground.

The last building occupied here was the post office, and it closed just after 1918. Pacific Springs is visible about one mile east of Highway 28.

PIEDMONT (Uinta)

This spot was originally the site of an Overland stage station. It had been built of stone, like some small fortress, to withstand Indian attacks. In 1857, the family of Moses Byrnes built a home here, probably sod at first. Charles Guild and his family joined them in 1864. Mrs. Guild and Mrs. Byrnes were sisters who came from

At ground level, at the front right-hand corner, some of these homes have small plaques with historical data. Others are missing their plaques because of theft. One of these homes was the residence of Willie Byrne from 1892 to 1940.

This is the Piedmont Cemetery.

The covered doorway of this building suggests that this structure might have been a church, school, or meeting hall.

Piedmont, Italy. This tiny community was called Byrne. As the railroad pushed west, tie camps were set up in the neighboring Uinta Mountains. These camps used Byrne as a supply center and weekend entertainment spot. When the Union Pacific Railroad came through in 1869 and built a station here, the place really boomed. It was later renamed Piedmont to avoid confusion with nearby Bryan. The economy of this town was based on five things: ranching, lumber, charcoal, the railroad, and soldiers from Fort Bridger. The town grew quickly. Soon, a general store, two-story hotel, school, post office, livery stable, newspaper, and a number of saloons to serve the troopers joined the railroad station. The population peaked in the 1870s at a little over two hundred people.

The charcoal in the West was usually used for smelting ore from one of the numerous mining booms. In this case, it was used for silver smelting in Utah. The wood for the kilns would have traveled a good distance from the Uinta Mountains to the southeast. Coal was known to exist in great quantity just north of here, but hostile Indians kept miners from developing deposits for decades. There was supposed to be an interpretive sign at the kilns, but during my visit in 2002, the sign was missing. Called beehive kilns because of their shape and appearance, this type of kiln was common in the West at one time.

There are three intact and one collapsed kiln here. A fifth had been dismantled and used as building material for a dam. Not long after Piedmont was established, coal began to pour from Wyoming mines, and the need for these kilns vanished. Beehive kilns may be found at numerous locations all over the West.

Next, Fort Bridger was closed, and most of the saloon business dried up with it. In 1901, the railroad built the Aspen tunnel north of the town. This was a shorter route, and the Union Pacific closed down the stretch of line Piedmont was on. By now, the town had shrunk to a population of around thirty-five. When the railroad left, Piedmont slowly faded until the last resident died in the 1940s. Today, the tracks are gone, but the old railroad bed is still there. Ranching became the area's sole industry.

This is a true ghost. Nobody lives here, but it is located on a working ranch, and visitors are not welcomed. The land is posted. A public road runs through the middle of the site though, allowing viewing and photo taking.

There are a couple of hazards here. When walking around, watch out for rattlesnakes and cow pies. While driving, watch for sheep and cattle on the road; there is a lot of livestock on this stretch to dodge. In bad weather, the road can be dangerous—especially the approach from the west. This portion of the road is an old railroad embankment. The sides are steep and in many cases more than ten feet higher than the surrounding ground. If you slide off this road, your vehicle will do a dangerous roll.

This small cluster of cabins was once a railroad boomtown.

Piedmont is shown on numerous atlases and maps, including the official state highway map, as a ghost town or historical site. Some of these sources only mention it as a location of kilns. Besides the kilns and railroad bed, there are a fair amount of remains here. Most of the buildings left were houses. There are structures on both sides of the road with the majority on the north side. Also, there is a barn that might have been part of the livery stable, but this is unconfirmed.

There are four houses in a neat row constructed of logs, lumber, railway ties, and mud stucco. They have small plaques at ground level at the front right-hand corner of the house. These might have been grave markers; in some burial practices, people are interred underneath a corner of the residence. These may also have just been historical markers. Whichever the case, most have been stolen, and the remaining ones show a great deal of age. One simply reads "Willie Byrne Home 1892–1940." This shows people lived here long after the town had given up the ghost. There is also a shed and two collapsed log structures.

On the south side are four additional structures. One building is collapsed with an intact peak roof sitting on top. The other three are still standing. One in the distance is a house. Another might have been the school; it has a separate roofed and walled doorway entrance. The last may have been a business or post office. Behind these buildings and the kilns is the Byrne-Hinsdale family cemetery. It rests on a gently sloping hill surrounded by sagebrush. It is obvious that the history of Piedmont and the Byrne family are intertwined.

The best way to reach Piedmont is from I-80. Take exit #24 and head south on a good gravel road. Piedmont is 7.5 miles down this

The larger lake in the photograph is Battle Lake. The town site of Rambler is located nearby.

road. The other route in from the west is more of an adventure. Take this road in dry weather only. This is the old railroad bed and has steep embankments. From State Highway 150, just south of Sulphur Springs Reservoir, turn east into Uinta County Road 173. While this route has its hazards, it is quite scenic.

RAMBLER (Carbon)

Rambler was one of seven copper boomtowns in the Sierra Madre. It is on the western side of Battle Pass just a few miles from the old town site of Battle. Information about its exact location is conflicting. Some sources show it right next to State Highway 70 at the top of the Battle Lake Basin while others have it at the bottom of the basin next to the lake. Both are probably correct. Mines and miners' shacks dotted the basin. Maps specifically show the Rambler mine, the main mining operation the town served, at the top of the basin. I have been to this spot and have seen the mine run-out and tailings. There are some wood foundations and a shack. This site is on the south side of Highway 70, almost astride the Continental Divide, and on private property.

The best and easiest way to view the remains of Rambler is to visit the museum in Encampment. The buildings shown here have been moved from various towns of the area's copper boom.

At the bottom of the basin was the likely town site itself. Some sources say a four-wheel-drive road can take you there; however, I did not locate this route on my maps or during hikes in the area. A steep trail takes you down to Battle Lake, but the hike back up is only for those in good physical condition. A good part of Rambler was built on a bog, and board walkways were used. The melting of the very large snow packs experienced here caused the bogs. Buildings in this part of town literally sank into the ground. Fragments may still be seen. There was said also to be an upper street on a side of a canyon. There are supposed to be some intact structures amongst a grove of aspen that hadn't been built on a bog.

The town of Rambler and its two principal mines, the Dane-Rambler and Ferris-Haggarty, were all started by the quartet of Ramsey, Deal, Ferris, and Haggarty. Probably the largest independent operation was the Joker Mine, located .7 of a mile south of the town near the lip of the basin at 9,620 feet. Rambler was one of the earliest of the Sierra Madre boomtowns; its origins date back to at least 1891. At its peak, its population was said to be in the hundreds. Copper was first mined here in 1879, but large quantities of ore weren't discovered until 1897.

This basin is avalanche country, a condition made worse by the miners. They stripped the mountainside's fir and pines and used the wood to build the towns, as support beams in the mines, as fuel for the smelters, and for cooking and heating. Of all the towns in this boom, Rambler had the worst avalanche problem.

Winter could be very hard because everything moved in and out by mule pack train. The Rambler mine at the top of the basin of course would not have had this problem. It was already out of the basin and located almost astride the main wagon road in the area. This was the road that ran to Battle Pass; this scenic road is Highway 70 today. Of course, the pass was often closed because of snow. Moreover, until they built the wagon road, a toll road, everything moved to Encampment by mule train. The basin is too deep and steep; it gives the area great beauty but makes avalanches and transportation a real problem. There must have been mines in the basin itself because numerous sources refer to ore being taken out of the town of Rambler at the bottom of the basin by the mule trains. There was no reason to haul ore down to Rambler, only to haul it back up. By the end of 1903, the ore hauled out of this place had produced four and a half million pounds of copper. A small amount was of very high grade, up to 51 percent pure metal.

In 1907, the mine company was working to extend the Encampment aerial tramway. At this point, the tramway was sixteen miles long and ran through the Rudefeha mine in Battle to the Ferris-Haggarty mine two miles farther west. The intent was to connect it to the Rambler mine and the mule train head at the top of the basin and run it into the basin. Also, the railroad line to Encampment was due to be completed during 1908.

When 1908 came, it was not the year for which everybody hoped and planned. The collapse of copper prices, fire, and stock fraud did everything in. Both the Haggarty and Rambler mines closed in 1908, and the company town closed with them. In the early 1900s, a mine called the "new Rambler" mined not only copper but a little bit of platinum group metals (PGM). The Wyoming State Geologic Society noted this in 1998 and also reported a renewed interest in exploration for these materials.

Best time to go is the summer; the place is usually snowed-in during the winter. Recent drought conditions over a vast portion of the West make many exceptions to the rule. The trip is not worth the effort to ghost town hunt, but it is worth the effort for the beauty and majestic setting.

RELIANCE (Sweetwater)

This is a semi-ghost that was established in 1910 as a coal-mining town, which started with the opening of the Reliance No. 1 mine. This was the name of the company and would become the name of the town. In fact, it became the name for everything here followed by either a number or the name of a pile of equipment. This was a company town.

A coal tipple was constructed here during 1910. A tipple is a large structure housing machinery that separates coal by size and loads it into wagons, trucks, or railway cars. The first one here was built of lumber, placed on a sandstone foundation, and called the Reliance Tipple. It operated from 1910 to 1936. Today, the foundation, a tailings pile, and assorted mining debris remind you of this place's true age. This lady can't lie.

In 1911, operations expanded, and three more mines, the Reliance No. 2, No. 3, and No. 4, started operations. By 1912, the location included four mine heads, the tipple, a railway spur, mine offices, a tramline, a warehouse, a hay barn, a lumberyard, a granary, scales, a post office, numerous cabins, and probably much more. Coal production continued to rise here until the end of World War I. By rough estimate, the peak population might have been around fifteen hundred.

After the end of the First World War, demand for coal dropped. The coming of the Great Depression accelerated this economic slide of the mining industry. To a town whose economy relied solely on coal mining, this was devastating. In 1936, a new mine and tipple were opened, both, of course, named Reliance. The Reliance No. 7 was located just east of town. The new tipple was a hulking steel-and-concrete structure. The new mine and tipple were modern, more productive, and cost efficient.

The return of some economic growth in the late 1930s increased demand. The coming of World War II caused demand to explode. By 1943, production was up to 1.4 million tons, and Reliance experienced a second boom. When World War II ended, coal production declined here. From the late 1940s until the mid-1950s, railroads, especially one of their largest customers, the Union Pacific, began to convert from coal-fired steam to diesel-electric locomotives. This was great for the railroads but a disaster to the coal industry. In 1955, the Reliance tipple and mines ceased production. The mines have never reopened. The tipple was abandoned and listed as a National Registered Historic Place on May 23, 1991. It looms today on a hillside silently looking over the town.

Today, Reliance has a post office and a population of around 330. The location is dotted with vacant buildings, homes, lots, and old mining equipment. Other sites worthy of investigation, such as East Plane, Gunn, Dines, Stansbury, and Winton, surround it. Be careful. Much property is private, many roads are rough, water is scarce, and rattlesnakes, wind, and dirt are plentiful.

This is the coal tipple in Reliance. It is a registered national historic landmark.

Reliance shows on the state highway map with an active rail line running to it. The location is easily accessible, and the route is well posted. The coal-mining ghost towns of Dines and Winton are just a few miles north. A study of maps shows Reliance to be sandwiched between the locations of Stansbury on the north and East Plane on the south. The same maps show an active rail line in the north and the southern route abandoned. This means the location of East Plane may bear checking out.

The environment is arid and harsh. Elevation is approximately 6,300 feet. To visit the sites around Reliance, one should have a detailed map, good tires, a four-wheel-drive vehicle, and plenty of water. To reach Reliance, head north from I-80 at the Rock Spring #104 exit. Take State Highway 191 for about three miles to Reliance Road. The town should be about another three miles east.

ROCK CREEK (Albany)
SITE NOT VISITED
This town started to die when the railroad moved west to present Rock River in 1901. The final nail in Rock Creek's coffin was when U.S. 30 (Lincoln Highway) was built and bypassed the town. The

final population was reportedly a family of four; they have since moved on. Currently, a local rancher owns the land, and permission to visit must be obtained from the landowner.

The road is a two-wheel drive (but rain can make it impassable). Snows can be heavy in the winter. Best time to visit, like almost all sites in the West, is the summer.

Rock Creek was founded in or around 1868 as a Union Pacific station on the transcontinental railroad. Over time, it became something of a shipping center. Mail was taken over land from here to Fort Fetterman. A stagecoach station began operating in 1870. During the 1880s, the government built a road through here, turning this into a freight wagon shipping point. Rock Creek made the headlines in June 1899 when one of the last big train robberies of the American frontier happened just west of town. The robbers stopped the train, separated the express car from the locomotive, and blew up the express car with dynamite. Then, they dynamited a bridge, forcing

Above: The loss of both railroad and highway traffic has caused the majority of Rock River's business district to become vacant.

Left: These are two out-of-business service stations from different time periods.

Opposite page, left: One-horsepower traffic was not an uncommon sight in town.

the engineer and locomotive to backtrack to Medicine Bow to report the robbery. It was first claimed the robbers were the Hole in the Wall Gang; this was probably true, but not proven. However, this did not keep Hollywood from using the scene in the movie, *Butch Cassidy and the Sundance Kid.*

For a while, this was one of Wyoming's premier Old West–style ghost towns. It was featured in many magazines and newspapers and even used as a Hollywood film set on a number of occasions. During the early 1990s, an arsonist destroyed most of this in a single evening. It is reported that there is mostly debris here now and also probably a cemetery. Additional information may be obtained at the Rock River Museum.

This was the town bank, and now it is a nice museum. A sign in the window offers a phone number to call if the facility is closed. If you call during business hours, someone will come and open the museum for you.

ROCK RIVER (Albany)

One of a number of ghost and semi-ghost towns strung out on Highway 287/30, this is a semi-ghost with a population listed as 235 by the 2000 census. A website says the population is 400, but a look at the place tells you this number is high. Often, the official census number will appear high because the city limits may include numerous outlying ranches and farms. Rock River looks like it had a population of 100 to 150.

After the lumber company closed, this structure was used as an antique store; that too has closed.

Like all the other towns on this stretch of road, Rock River got its start as a Union Pacific Railroad town. The Union Pacific moved its tracks a couple of miles west from the town of Rock Creek to this present location of Rock River. The town is very much like Medicine Bow, only smaller. It was founded in 1900 and incorporated in 1909. When the Lincoln Highway (Highway 30) was built, it bypassed Rock Creek and ran through Rock River, which killed Rock Creek. During Rock Creek's slow demise, most of its population moved to Rock River. When I-80 was constructed, it ran south of Medicine Bow, bypassing the Lincoln Highway route and its string of towns. By this time, the Union Pacific still ran next to the town but no longer stopped here. Now it was Rock River's turn for a slow decline.

The stream of Rock Creek flows about a mile south. Elevation is listed as 6,892 feet. The business district of the town is almost entirely deserted; only three businesses are currently open: a bar, gas station, and combination café/motel. At least a dozen other businesses are vacant. These vacant buildings date from the early 1900s to the 1970s. Some have obviously been modernized and rebuilt over time, but their false fronts still show.

The First National Bank building was renovated during the summer of 1996 and converted into the Rock River Museum. During my last visit, there was a sign on the front door with instructions to call for someone to open the museum. That person arrived within a few minutes of my call. It is worth the wait if you want to visit, which we did. The museum has displays covering several areas from dinosaurs to the pioneer days. The exhibits occupy not just the old bank but also the town's one-time library.

Just about everyone in town is using some old building for something other than its original purpose. A rancher at the edge of town is using an old motel for storage. Part of the old Lincoln Hotel has been converted into a house. There is a vacant false front building next door that may be an older part of the hotel. There is supposed to be a 1928 concrete Lincoln Highway marker here, and

another is reportedly located on Fourth Street. The museum and
the old hotel are both on Avenue C. There once was another bank
in town. All that's left of it is the old bank vault, which someone is
using as a storage shed. About half the homes appear to be vacant.
The Lincoln Highway bisects the town.

RUDEFEHA (Carbon)
SITE NOT VISITED

Rudefeha was a company mining town and home of the "Battle"
copper mine. Another mine near here was the Ferris-Haggarty.
The town got its name from an amalgamation of the owners'
names: J. M. Rumsey, Robert Deal, George Ferris, and Ed Haggarty.
Ed Haggarty actually located this site and the Rudefeha Mine
site at Battle, Wyoming, during the spring of 1897. He had been
"grubstaked" by the other three men and went prospecting to locate
marketable quantities of copper ore. Copper was already mined in
small quantities in the area. The small but focused expedition led to
a mining boom.

The ore from these mines was sent down to the smelter in
Encampment. When mine owners closed the saloons in town, the
bar owners simply moved a mile west and set up a new town called
Dillon. This second establishment soon grew to be the largest town
in the Sierra Madre. After less than a decade, the ore veins grew
small and copper prices dropped. The Battle mine closed in 1907 and
the Ferris-Haggarty in 1908, along with the company town.

There are unconfirmed remains accessible by four-wheel-drive
vehicle on National Forest Road 862, although the area is impassable
in winter. The ruins of Copperton and Dillon are nearby.

SAGE (Lincoln)

Located on a windswept desert prairie, this is a great and little-
reported ghost. I found just one mention of the town on the
Internet, and it is shown on the official state highway map. All other
information came from actually visiting the site.

Top: This is the part of Sage that is immediately
adjacent to the highway.

Bottom: As posted, this building is dangerous, and
entrance should not be attempted.

It was an interesting but hot July visit. Parts of the town site were posted and fenced off. I respected the postings, of course, which made research even more challenging. For instance, I noticed two cemeteries enclosed with wooden fences but could not examine them because they rested on the posted part of the site.

Sage was once a stop on the Union Pacific Railroad, and the company had a train station there. The UP no longer makes regular stops here, and the depot is gone. Cattle or sheep were shipped from here. Livestock pens dot the community, and there is a large

Above: The square-cut timbers on this structure reveal it to be of older construction than most other buildings in town.

Left: Many of the vacant homes are boarded up like these.

Opposite page, top: At first, it is hard to tell if this sign is pointing to a community or just all the nearby sagebrush.

Opposite page, bottom: The ramp in the distance was used for loading livestock into railcars.

earthen ramp next to an unused railroad siding. The large number of abandoned farm implements shows this place was also an agricultural community. The name for this deceased town simply comes from the dominating feature—sage plants.

Today, Sage is populated by a family or two who occupy a few of the buildings and trailers. About a dozen buildings are vacant; their construction and condition vary greatly. Debris piles and stone foundations show where many buildings once stood. By examining the different types of construction, you can tell this place was first occupied well before the start of the twentieth century, and construction continued until the 1930s. One building from the 1970s sits boarded up next to the highway. There are at least two cemeteries, a number of streets, the old railroad siding with earthen loading ramp, and numerous sheds and pens, all easily visible. More buildings tantalizingly dot the near horizon. In and around all of this is, of course, sagebrush.

Sage is very hot in the summer, bitterly cold in the winter, and devoid of any protection from wind or sun. The ground is level, so the elevation of 6,332 feet shouldn't matter. Be wary of rattlesnakes. Sage rests quietly on the south side of Highway 30 about twenty-four miles west of Kemmerer. A sign on the highway points to the site. The question is why?

SHELL (Bighorn)

Everything here is named Shell. There is Shell Canyon, Shell Canal, Shell Creek, Shell Falls, and the town. The owner of the Old Shell Lodge says the name comes from the large amount of fossilized shells encased in the area rock. This town is more of a sleeper than a ghost. There are two businesses that are open off and on. The locals are friendly but independent-minded. On my first visit through, signs said "open" but neither business was. During a follow-up phone call, I was informed that these business concerns were opened on "a felt-like-it basis." On the other hand, I was invited for dinner. When I asked if the lodge had a restaurant, I was told it did

Additional buildings and old farm equipment were scattered over the countryside. These are beyond the posted fence, so respect private property and view from a distance.

but doesn't now, yet he offered to cook a cheeseburger. Even if his answers were less than definite, the owner was helpful, friendly, and sincere. He even called back to again extend his invitation to a meal on my next pass through town.

The Old Shell Lodge was built in 1890 and is of stone construction. This is a one-and-one-half-story structure with a false front. Across the street are a string of small stone cabins and a café. The café is a chalet-style building with stone façade. It appears that at one time it served as a gas station. Nearby is the Shell store, which was built in 1902 and operates off and on. This is a beautiful little town with

Above: This is Shell Falls, a major area attraction.

Left: These beautiful and unique buildings house businesses that are open on an off-and-on basis.

interesting architecture. If these businesses are open, it is a sleepy community. If they are closed, it is a semi-ghost.

Shell, founded in 1886, is bisected by Highway 14 at the western entrance to beautiful Shell Canyon. At 4,210 feet, elevation is low by Wyoming standards. A post office serves the population of about fifty. On Smith Avenue is the Shell Community Church, built in 1903. Next to the church is the Shell Community Hall, which was constructed over 1933–34 under the Depression CWA Program. They are built of local material including huge logs from the Big Horn Mountains. Both of these buildings are still in use today. The historic Red Shell Schoolhouse, just south of here, ceased being used after 1989. The drive through Shell Canyon is extremely scenic. Nearby Shell Falls has a visitor's center and is a worthwhile stop.

SILVER CLIFF/NEW ROCHELLE/RUNNING WATER (Niobrara)
SITE NOT VISITED

This location is on Mining Hill, one mile west of the town of Lusk. For three different generations, various people tried to make a profit from a silver-and-radium-bearing ore here. A bustling town and stagecoach stop boomed from 1879 to 1886. When the bust came, most buildings were moved to Lusk. Small profits and a number of reported litigations stopped the mining eventually. Remains are said to be scant.

SILVER CROWN (Laramie)
SITE NOT VISITED

This site is marked on numerous highway atlases (some as late as 2002) as a ghost town location. I don't think it is anymore or that it has been for quite a while. This may be a case of old data just being taken for granted and copied. I studied detailed maps, drove through the area, and talked with locals but found no evidence, remains, or history of the town.

I finally located its history in a book from 1956. The town started in 1885 as a gold rush. But the sample lode of ore turned out to be salted; it had been a hoax. During the same time though, it was discovered that the ore contained a small amount of silver. The boom continued for only a short while; the ore was low grade. With nearby Hecla, the whole area is called the Silver Crown Hills. The site is on private property, and there may be little or no remains.

SOUTH PASS CITY (Fremont)

This is a little side trip that won't disappoint. A short journey down a dirt road from a remote two-lane highway is the State Historic Site of South Pass City. Named for nearby historic South Pass, this is the fraternal twin of Atlantic City. An easy ascent across the Continental Divide, this was an important destination for those using the Oregon Trail. Nearly a half million emigrants crossed here between 1843 and 1912 when the last recorded wagon rolled through. The wagon ruts and grooves of some that used this trail are still nearby.

To visit South Pass City is to step back in time.

At first, people mostly passed through. Then in the summer of 1867 came the cry of gold! The Carissa Mine opened first, followed by the founding of South Pass City. Soon the rush was on. By 1868, Atlantic City and Miners Delight were booming. South Pass City quickly grew to twenty-eight mines, three hundred buildings, and three thousand people. For a very short while, this was the largest city in Wyoming. Gold had been known to be in the area since at least 1842, but finding a worthwhile amount without being found by hostile Indians had been a definite challenge.

The first gold was discovered by panning in Sweetwater Creek. Attacking Arapaho, Cheyenne, and Sioux warriors forced miners to keep lookouts on hills. The miners left and didn't return in force until 1866 when troops arrived in the area. Even with the troops' presence, Indian attacks were frequent and heavy, and by 1869, they were a serious problem. But the miners had brought their families with them, and much equipment had been invested. There was no turning back this time. The Army would see to that.

When this place was finally able to grow, the bloom did not last long. Except for the Carissa Mine, no really large deposit was discovered and this soon petered out. Within two years, the population peaked at four thousand. Within five years, it was down to less than one hundred. The departing residents even took many of their buildings with them. The nearby army post, Camp Stambauch, closed in 1880. South Pass City hung on until 1912, servicing emigrants on the Oregon Trail and prospectors that still panned in the area. Even with the trail, the town was nearly deserted in 1880.

Many additional mine booms erupted from time to time. The dredge operation over at adjoining Rock Creek was a temporary shot in the arm. There was also a large hydraulic operation, a copper mine, and a strip mine. Panning never stopped in the area, and once in a while, one of the old mines reopened. This led to small booms in the 1880s, 1890s, and 1930s. During this time, the population would fluctuate from a handful to as many as five hundred people.

A fair number of structures here have been beautifully restored to their original appearance.

Today, half the town is a park and the other half a cottage community. The park is a State Historic Site and charges admission. It is worth the price. The park is seasonably open from May 15 through October 15. There are over thirty original buildings in restored condition. Two, a general store and a saloon, are even open for business. The general store is a gift and sweets shop. The saloon has the original billiards table and serves nonalcoholic frontier-day drinks, root beer and sarsaparilla.

The cottage half of the town has some additional original buildings. Some of the homes are occupied all year and others just seasonally—satellite dishes are common. A Masonic Lodge has been placed in the privately reconstructed Freund Brothers Gun Shop. Some of the cabins or their outbuildings are from the boom periods, but most are from more recent times.

South Pass City is on a dirt road east of Wyoming State Highway 28. There are two turnoffs, one from the north and one from the south. Both are well marked. Stay on this road unless you have a local topographic map, or you might get lost. This is 34 miles southwest of Lander and 4.5 miles southwest of Atlantic City.

STANSBURY (Sweetwater)
SITE NOT VISITED

I found this mining ghost sandwiched between Reliance and Dines while doing map studies. It showed at the end of both a rail line and road spur with mines around it. I could find no evidence of a current town by its name in the state of Wyoming, so this is probably a ghost. A telephone call to the Reliance post office revealed that Stansbury was a coal-mining town. It was named for a man who surveyed the area in the 1840s and 1850s for the coal-mining industry.

There were unconfirmed plans to reopen the mine here in the spring of 2005. Upon my visit to the area then, it had not yet opened. Structures and mine equipment are kept in serviceable condition. Stansbury is located on private property. It sounds like a town that is asleep, just waiting for spring to come out of its hibernation.

Above: Mines were in and all around the town.

Left: This is a restored one-room schoolhouse.

Stansbury is located about three air miles north of Reliance. It can be reached by heading north on Winton Road. Turn right onto the first road-and-railway-spur combination after Reliance. Stansbury lies one mile east on this dead-end spur. Unnamed and mismarked roads abound in the area. A detailed map and local directions are recommended.

SUBLETTE (Lincoln)
SITE NOT VISITED

These are the remains of a coal-mining town named for the famous Sublette brothers. There are no residents, and remains are scattered over a wide area. The environment is arid and harsh. There is no shade, and rain can bring flash floods. Watch for rattlesnakes. An old railroad bed and a four-wheel-drive road lead to the site.

In 1857, a shortcut was established in southwest Wyoming on the Oregon Trail, known as the Sublette Cutoff. A traveler's town by the name of Sublette sprang up that year. The Sublette brothers had helped blaze the trail in the 1820s. Cattle and the railroad followed in the next two decades. Sublette had its last boom circa 1890s as a coal-mining town. There are other coal-mining towns nearby, such as Diamondville, Kemmerer, and Opal, and historically they have much in common with Sublette's last boom.

The remains consist mostly of foundations and old mining equipment. A couple of buildings are still intact; the best is an old jail. The few buildings that are left were constructed of stone. It was the only building material besides adobe that would have been available in this desert environment. Sublette may be found approximately five miles north and slightly west of Kemmerer. The best season to visit, even though it can be hot, is summer. Elevation is approximately 7,000 feet.

SUNRISE (Platte)

Sunrise was a company mine town, emphasis on *was*. As late as 1984, this place was a complete town with a skeleton caretaker crew. Today, this past iron ore mining operation is mostly rows of tiered

One of several rather long automotive garages, this one even contains a few antique automobiles.

foundations. Since it is located on posted private property, I am puzzled by its appearance on the most recent state highway map. On my visit, I was very fortunate to meet a kindly gentleman by the name of Mr. Jesus J. Rodriguez, who was born in neighboring Hartville and worked various jobs with the mine at Sunrise for twenty-seven years.

Mr. Rodriguez had a key and permission from the owner to enter the land. First, this gracious man gave me a tour of his unique and beautiful garden. Next, he gave me the tour and history of the old town of Hartville. After all that, he rode in my van up the old state highway spur to Sunrise. There, he gave me another guided walking tour and history lecture. He spent half the day with me. It was a great half-day!

Although the majority of buildings have been torn down, there is still much to view at Sunrise. This site was large and well developed.

Above: This building once served as the mine's headquarters and workers' recreation center at the Sunrise Mine.

Right: This is old farm equipment that the current landowner has been collecting.

Steep valley walls pinched the place and squeezed the town tight. Mining operations started before 1920 and were both shaft and pit types. Operations ceased on June 30, 1980, owing to lack of profitability. There is still plenty of iron ore there. It had been hoped another mining company would restart operations, but this failed to materialize. Operating costs here had become too high. These were "wet" mines and had to be pumped of water constantly.

Because Sunrise was a company town, it had a little of everything, except saloons. There was a hotel, post office, gas station, automotive repair garage, mercantile, school, doctor's office, fire department, and more. Numerous fire hydrants sticking up from sagebrush hint at busier days. The main mine office building, which is still standing, doubled as a community center. It had a poolroom for the miners, a YMCA for the town's children, and in the basement, Wyoming's first bowling alley. People used to come from miles around just to see it. The mining operation had its own standard-gauge railroad. This was a spur that the company used to move the ore down to the feeder line in neighboring Hartville. The railroad bed is still there, but the tracks were ripped up in the mid-1980s. The railroad still shows on some current maps, but trust me, it's gone.

Most of the workers' quarters were frame-and-tarpaper row houses, only twenty feet apart. Most have been burned down to avoid property tax assessment, and only foundations and yards are visible. The yards are fenced in by low, rough-hewn, stone walls and full of aging fruit trees. The miners and their families planted the plum, peach, apple, and chokecherry trees. Residents also grew grapes on the hillside and made wine. Duplex-style brick homes still stand here. These provided housing for the company doctor, supervisors, mine company officers, etc.

Many of the mine buildings—large concrete, steel, and red brick structures—are still standing. They include the hoist room, a power plant, machinery shops, and a large shower house. Mr. Rodriguez walked me through this building and told me the story of how he bathed in the creek until he reached the age of eighteen and worked at the mine. Here, at the Sunrise mine, he experienced his first shower. He was always the last one out—sometimes, not until a foreman rousted him out.

At one time, this location had a wooden frame auto garage that was 136 stalls long. It was featured in an edition of *Ripley's Believe It or Not*, and the long concrete foundation is still there. The number of

Left: This street is lined with the yards and foundations of the homes that used to belong to the miners.

Top: This was once the home of the company doctor. Brick homes were reserved for section employees and management. Many of these still stand.

Bottom: The building at the upper left corner housed the engines that operated the mine lifts.

additional intact buildings and large, deep foundations is beyond the scope of this work. As much as had been removed by time and man, there was still too much to describe. But most won't get to see it unless they're lucky and get a tour like I did. Most people will see only what's at the front gate. There is a large, intact garage with the year 1920 boldly carved into stone just before you get to the gate. On the other side of the gate, you see current ranching structures and two wrecked company buildings. This was the mine headquarters. An abandoned railbed follows the road on the left, and building foundations follow the road on the right all the way from Hartville. Many of these foundations are rather large and give a good indication how developed this place was. At least one of these foundations was the Hartville/Sunrise school. Most of what there is to see intact lays beyond the locked gate. Once again, this is posted private property.

The current owner is using the property for a horse ranch but has additional plans. Some claim he intends to make a historical museum of part of the site. He also hopes to sell mine waste to a cement plant in Laramie. The EPA was studying the matter at the time of my visit. Hartville residents are concerned about heavy metals and other mining wastes in the dirt the trucks would haul right down Main Street. They fear dust from the hauling operation might contaminate their area.

This is a semi-arid environment. It is hot in the summer (at least it was on my early June visit) and cold in the winter. This is also rattlesnake country—wear boots.

Sunrise is just east and uphill from Hartville at the end of State Route 318.

This is the actual mine itself. There is still plenty of ore here; it's just too expensive to retrieve.

ghost towns of wyoming

SUPERIOR (Sweetwater)

This was a coal-mining town. Just after 1900, prospecting showed sufficient reserves to warrant development along a dry wash known as Horse Thief Creek. A railroad survey was conducted up the long canyon from Thayer Junction on the main Union Pacific line. In the meantime, mine locations were designated and a town site planned. Digging started on October 23, 1903, at the "C" mine.

At this point, the town was known as Reliance. To gain capitalization for further development, the company went public on December 28, 1905. It was registered as the Superior Coal Company with a capital stock of ten thousand shares with a par value of one hundred dollars a share—obviously not a poor man's stock for the time.

The building on the left contained pumps and compressors. The one on the right was the miners' shower house, the same shower house Mr. Rodriguez enjoyed so much.

On July 14, 1906, the town's name was changed to Superior, for the company that built it. During the same year, "A", "B", and "D" mines were opened. During 1910, "E" mine was opened, and a modern steel screening plant was built. A gas producer plant was installed at the "D" mine to operate an electric generator, but it was inefficient and removed in 1922. Depleted reserves shut down the "E" mine in 1937.

This community was at its heyday between 1910 and 1920. The population probably peaked in 1920 when it reached 1,580. The town had a bank, a hotel, a hospital, a school, a post office, and, a rarity for central Wyoming, an opera house. The large United Mine Workers building contained the union hall and offices, a dance hall, a grocery store, a bowling alley, a doctor's office, a dentist's office, and the only saloon I found. In the center of town was a railway

Top and middle: This was the miners' union hall. Today, it is an open-air museum.

Bottom: This was Superior's main business district.

Right: The town still maintains a small, beautiful park.

depot and additional retail establishments. Mining communities in such harsh and isolated environments needed to be as self-contained as possible.

The largest blow to Superior was the Great Depression. This economic calamity hit rural and western America before it befell the eastern cities. By the 1930 census, Superior's population dropped to 241. It has not rebounded since.

In 1934, it became evident that the coal reserves of the Superior mines were nearing exhaustion. The only thing to do was find more coal, so prospecting was conducted on a vigorous basis. By 1936, new reserves had been discovered. These were developed, and a new mine, the D. O. Clark mine, named for a western coal industry pioneer, was opened on January 1, 1939. For its day, it was an extremely modern operation. Two independent mines not owned by the Superior Coal Company, the Premier and Copenhagen mines, also opened around this time.

Different means were used to haul the coal to the surface. Early on, mules were the most common method. The haulage from two seams was done by an endless rope haulage on an outside plane to the tipple. Another means was by small electric locomotives. These

ghost towns of wyoming

Left: During the town's boom period, the Alberta Hotel was claimed the best place to stay.

Below: Housing types and material vary greatly, but much of it was obviously company housing.

became more common with the passage of time, but use of the mules never completely stopped.

Immigrant labor from numerous European countries and Japan were prominent. Japanese lived in their own community, known locally as "the Japanese Village." It was located south of South Superior, an independent community south of Superior. It was a place for people who did not belong to or want to be in "the company town." Today, there are no remains of either the Japanese Village or South Superior.

The Superior mines were relatively safe for the time and won awards for their safety record. People still live here; the 2000 census says the population is 244, but there are no services. This is a virtually treeless, high altitude (about 6,000 feet), desert plateau, and the weather matches it. The place is very hot in the summer, cold in the winter, and often windy.

Iron ore was also mined in some quantities. The ore was milled into pellets and then shipped by rail to Rock Springs. Iron ore mining ceased in the area during the 1970s.

Superior is nine miles north of I-80's exit #122 at the end of Wyoming 371. Along the way, you'll notice the old railroad bed and

numerous tresses that crossed the zigzagging Horse Thief Creek. The tracks have long since been ripped up and hauled away.

There is a lot to see. The railroad depot has been converted into a house and subsequently vacated again. The miners' union hall is gutted but standing and converted to an open-air museum, a must-see in Superior. Across the street is a small attractive city park complete with picnic benches, a Union Pacific caboose, and about the only grass I saw in town. The City Hall is an old, red brick building. It is still in use and also houses the town fire department. Main Street is paved and flanked by many boarded-up vacant businesses, including the bank, the Alberta Hotel, and a store called the Working Men Commercial Company. I found no saloons, but since this was a company town, there probably never were any other than the one in the miners' union hall. This was most likely the main function of South Superior. There had been a school and a cemetery in Superior, but I located neither.

Uniquely, there are no false-front buildings in this Western town. The housing is very mixed. Most are vacant, but you can't come to that conclusion merely by their appearance. Some are obvious company cookie-cutter houses set in straight lines while a handful have rather ornate exteriors. Many houses were built on the hillsides overlooking the town. By examining construction materials and techniques, you can see building went on here over at least a forty-year period. There are collapsed log structures as well as homes with asbestos siding. In fact, every material but marble appears to have been used to construct the homes and businesses. The side roads are not paved and have out-of-use fire hydrants. Most of the frame homes are built on stone foundations while a couple of houses were built entirely of local rock. In more recent times, mobile homes have been dispersed throughout the town. These are occupied. The 2000 census claims a population of 256 for this community.

Two miles north of town is an area of petrified wood. It is on the right side of the road and at first seems to be nothing more than a

Two types of building construction are shown at Tinton. The one with tarpaper roof and thinly framed walls represents those used for workers' housing and service buildings such as the company store and the post office. The second type, with shingled roof and brick walls, was housing for supervisors and managers.

This was supposed to have been one of the main business streets of Tinton.

big pile of black rock. Good samples, some quite large but brittle. I do not know when the mines closed, but closed they are. This was most likely owing to the coal seams pinching out.

TINTON (Crook)

This town is located on the South Dakota–Wyoming state border with the borderline supposedly running up and down Main Street. Websites display a photo of a grass-covered street with frame buildings on both sides and claim this is Main Street. Trouble is, this street runs east–west and the South Dakota–Wyoming border runs north–south. National Forest Road 222, from which you view the town, was the main road that divided the town between the two states. Today, all buildings on the Wyoming side have been replaced by the latest mining operation. The blacksmith shop, post office, school, hotel, and other parts of the town's business section were here until demolished in 1996. Tinton is a photographer's dream and probably the best ghost town of the Black Hills.

Tinton got its start as a placer gold–mining town in 1876, but the ore deposits were not extensive and were soon exhausted. Tinton

The vault of this building could have belonged to a bank or a butcher shop.

As yet unconfirmed, this is reported to be part of Roosevelt Square.

almost faded from existence, but the Black Hills tin rush revived it. Placer tin had been known to be in the area since 1876, and in 1884, a hard-rock tin strike was made. This was a boomer, and by 1904, a company-type town had been built by the Tinton Company. Most of the buildings there now are from this period.

During its tin production phase, Tinton became the "classic" company mining town. Several different mining companies, including the Boston Tin Company, the American Tin Plate Company, the Tinton Company, and the Tinton Reduction Company, owned the town. These companies not only ran the town, they "were" the town. You can see this still today, down to the company store.

The mine closed down during the early 1930s but was partially replaced by a sawmill. The town also had an operating school with eight grades in two rooms and a general store. Tin mining resumed periodically until the 1950s, and just before World War II, the government did a lot of test drilling and tunneling in a mineral survey. Other rock minerals discovered have been columbite, tantalite, and amblygonite.

Today, the town consists of a miners' hall, a post office, a store complete with company sign, and about ten homes lining both sides of Main Street. Mining structures and debris occupy much area around the town. Many more houses are downhill and out of sight from the road. The housing stock is mixed. Miners' homes were frame and tarpaper construction or built of rough-hewn lumber. Homes with plaster walls and shingled roofs belonged, obviously, to management, supervisors, and company owners. Some of these houses even had wood or concrete sidewalks. A fallen tree had heavily damaged a house just east of this location. The story is that some loggers felled the tree onto the structure just for the fun of it. Supposedly, this was a house for "soiled doves." Miners would have had to leave a company town like Tinton to obtain certain services.

Getting to Tinton requires a topographic map and a good vehicle or the will to take a long hike. Any route you choose will go through very scenic and rugged country. The best way to drive in is from the South Dakota side on Forest Service Road 222. According to the route you take and source you use, there are several ghost towns along the way. An often-suggested route lies at the very back of Spearfish Canyon and proceeds for six miles west of Iron Creek. In the winter, the roads may be snowed in.

Time forgot about Tinton for a while. By around 1940, local hunters were using it as a spot to hunt deer. Today, the town is fenced and posted. The photos of Tinton that appear on the Internet are taken from the road that runs through the site.

The current property owner is commercial miner Tinton Enterprises, which presently mines a mineral called tantalum. Tantalum is a refractory metal with many uses, including nuclear weapons components. Supposedly, the material being mined here is used to make dinner china. This company mines seasonally. In the winter, they work around Deadwood. During the summer, the Tinton operation is worked.

Top: This is part of the current mining operation at Tinton. It is located on the Wyoming part of the site and has consumed a number of original structures such as the old mill.

Bottom: As viewed from the road, the old homes were numerous and disappeared into the woods.

In the center of this and out of sight from the road is Roosevelt Square. It has been said that Kermit Roosevelt, son of Teddy, spent the winter of 1920 in Tinton. Residents named the square "Roosevelt" in his honor. Including the ones that are collapsed, there are probably thirty to forty buildings in this part of town.

Locals pronounce this place Tint-In and correct you if you don't pronounce it as such. Some of the information used for this location was obtained from a man who wandered into my camp. He claims he was Tinton's winter caretaker for thirteen years.

A few miles southwest, in Crook County, Wyoming, is Mineral Hill, another ghost town location.

TRAILTOWN (Park)
SITE NOT VISITED

This is a tourist attraction located on the original site of Cody. It is a collection of old buildings and artifacts, even Butch Cassidy and the Sundance Kid's "Hole in the Wall" cabin. There are twenty-five other restored buildings, dating from 1879 to 1901, collected from ghost towns located all over the state of Wyoming. There is a cabin built by Victor Arland and moved from the town that bore his name. The Rivers Saloon still has bullet holes in its door! Many of the buildings are stocked with items of the era, and a museum here is loaded with Indian and pioneering artifacts. Sometimes referred to as Old Trailtown, its location is two miles west of Cody on U.S. 14/16/20. An admission fee is charged.

TUBB TOWN/FIELD CITY (Weston)

Approximately four miles east of Newcastle and the junction of U.S. Highways 85 and 16 are the ruins of Tubb Town. One of eight Wyoming Black Hills ghosts, it was an attempted railroad town on the western edge of the Black Hills that got started in the spring of 1889. It was a modest beginning. DeLoss Tubbs of Custer, South Dakota, built and operated a store here in the place named Field City by Tubbs but called Tubb Town by everybody else. The town was built on the gamble that the railroad would choose this area for

If you follow the highway map to the location of Tubb Town, it will take you to this sign. All the original buildings have since been moved to Newcastle, Wyoming.

its next line, and it was alleged to have few laws and many saloons. Like other western locations, Tubb Town claims Calamity Jane as a visitor. She was known to have lived and worked in the Black Hills at this time, so there may be something to this claim.

The discovery of coal at Cambria enabled the Burlington and Missouri River Railroad to come farther west. Tubbs and other businessmen became "boomers" and laid out Field City along Salt Creek. The city's backers demanded far too high a price for the land, and in November, the railroad rerouted two miles farther west. This made Newcastle a boomtown and Field City a stillbirth. Residents quickly gave up the ghost and moved to Newcastle, taking even their buildings with them. Tubb Town was born and died in the same year.

Since the residents took their buildings with them, one may wonder why Tubb Town appears on numerous maps and atlases as a ghost town location. There are two reasons for this. First, there is a Wyoming historical marker dedicated to Field City at the original site along Highway 16. Second, there was an attempt to create a tourist ghost town, and its remains are located here.

Al Smith, founder of the Accidental Oil operation, attempted a tourist attraction just west of the historical marker. Buildings were bought from Newcastle, disassembled, and moved to tourist Tubb

Top: This is one of the buildings moved back from Newcastle for the attempted tourist attraction named Tubb Town.

Bottom: This is a shepherd's wagon brought to "tourist" Tubb Town. It currently rests on Accidental Oil's back lot, ironically the actual site of the original Tubb Town.

Left: The original location of Tubb Town lies just beyond this billboard.

Top: These are buildings from Newcastle that were disassembled, awaiting reassembly for the "tourist" Tubb Town.

Bottom: This is one of a handful of structures erected for the "tourist" Tubb Town. These buildings are all on private property.

Town. The endeavor was not a success. Most of the buildings date from the 1920s, and two remain on private property on the north side of Highway 16. More buildings are kept in the back storage lot of Accidental Oil where some lie as stacks of lumber. They had been disassembled but, like "Humpty Dumpty," never put back together again. One structure appears to have been a sheepherder's wagon.

Ironically, this is actually the old location of Tubb Town. Permission to enter may be obtained at the Visitor's Center of Accidental Oil. Tubb Town is located on the northern side of Highway 16, 7.9 miles west of the South Dakota–Wyoming state border.

Accidental Oil is a museum and an unusual off-and-on oil operation, not a ghost town. This is a tourist operation with narrated tours during which you are led to the original hand-dug well. These walking tours are informative and usually conducted by a member of the friendly Smith family. A small fee is charged for this service. Parking, the outdoor museum, and admission to the gift shop are free. Its appearance is more of an abandoned oil operation than that of a museum. There is much old oil-drilling equipment here, some dating back to the 1880s. One drilling rig is from the infamous Teapot Dome. This is a great place to see the history of the oil industry in Wyoming. It covers a fair area at this location, and there is no shade.

This site's oil operation was much newer than most of the equipment on display here at the museum. The name Accidental Oil is a misnomer; this is a planned operation. The oil here was found at a very shallow depth—a mere twenty-four feet. Al Smith, a lifelong oilman, wildcatted this site in 1966. He leased the land from the government, and when he couldn't move a drilling rig onto the property before the lease ran out, he literally dug a well with pick and shovel. After only a month of digging, he struck oil. The well's peak production, if indeed it could be called that, was five barrels of crude a day. This is not refinable oil but rather an industrial-type lubricant. On my last visit, production was down to less than a barrel a day, and there was no buyer for the commodity.

Alongside the museum of equipment, there is a viewing room so that one can look at the seepage process. This is the actual well that Smith dug. There is also an unusual gift shop. The owners have converted a ten-thousand-barrel, sixty-five-foot diameter, oil storage tank into their store. It is open daily from Memorial Day to Labor Day. The location is easy to find and offers convenient access on and off the highway. It is an informative and interesting stop. Their website is: *http://w3.trib.com/~debran/index.html*.

VACATION RANCH (Park)

This is a vacant vacation ranch, but the location has not been abandoned. An important distinction between vacant and abandoned is that one is physical and the other is legal. At the time of my visit, the Forest Service denied vehicular access to the ranch. It has condemned several bridges on the road to the ranch. The initial bridge has been gated and bears a sign noting the route's closure to vehicle traffic, effectively closing down the business. The owner of the ranch is reportedly contesting the government's action in court. The campground host provided this information as well as the route to the site.

To keep visitation down, I will intentionally omit the specific campground name. For one reason, the site is vacant and in contention, not abandoned. Second, the site, including the structures and the land that encompasses them, is pristine. Third, the hike in requires one to walk through active grizzly and cougar territory. Both the forest ranger and campground host were insistent that I carry bear spray. Not owning any and being thickheaded, I informed them I intended to hike in the morning without it. Because a cougar and grizzly, both with cubs, were currently very active in the area, the campground host lent me his bear spray, and the ranger made sure that I signed out in the morning and signed in upon returning. My hiking route for the day ran through the center of the animals' territory, so I made lots of noise on this solo hike. Surprisingly, a grizzly with cubs was not on the day's agenda.

Although no signs of the cougar or grizzly were seen, the remains of a mauled bobcat were spotted in a tree.

I did have a wildlife experience, but it was in camp, not on the hike. It involved bighorn sheep and my desire to get a good picture. At one point, the dominant male of the group expressed his wish to have more personal space, which means he charged me. In return, I demonstrated my overwhelming passion for large flora; that is, I got behind a big tree. By the third tree, he was content, and I had my photos.

The dirt road to the ranch can be rough and narrow. Wet weather would make it tough going in the family car, but the bridge closures render the point moot. The road leads up a small valley that it shares

Above: This is your first view of the ranch after a three-hour hike.

Opposite page, top: This was the main lodge.

This page and opposite, sides: There are a small number of various beautiful cabins here.

with a meandering stream. This makes for a beautiful setting but also leads to the need for bridges as the stream repeatedly cuts across the path of the road.

The environment is semi-arid with scattered stands of pines on the mountainsides. Along the stream are numerous species of trees, shrubs, and large bushes. Sagebrush and prairie grass fill the spaces in between. The large brush growth, particularly at river crossings and certain bends in the road, were ideal spots for accidental contact or even animal ambush. The mountains rise up in front and to both sides of you. Wildlife is abundant and the scenery spectacular. Even in late June, the peaks were capped in white.

I am uncertain of the mileage, but it was a three-hour hike, one way. As for the bridges, they were in fine condition to walk across. I am not qualified to comment on their condition for vehicular traffic; the Army only taught me how to blow them up. Also, there were numerous signposts along the road—just posts; the signs had all been removed.

Once there, you find yourself in a setting Hollywood would envy. Pine pole fencing surrounds the location. Trees are thicker at this higher altitude and provide welcome shade. Cabins are constructed of logs with covered porches and stone chimneys. Besides the cabins, there is a two-story house and a small lodge. All buildings are done in the classic Western style. The location is relatively flat but dominated on three sides by high rugged ground. The site slopes toward the fourth side and opens up, revealing a view of snow-capped peaks in the distance. This place is wrapped in natural beauty, and the cabins don't scar the land but rather blend into it. While it may not be a ghost, it was truly asleep. Not a soul was there, but firewood was still stacked on the front porches, just waiting for the next visitor who liked cool mountain nights and stone fireplaces.

Above: Looking back on the hike to Vacation Ranch.

Top left: Having already been warned by the ranger about aggressive cougars and grizzlies in the area, this dead bobcat in the tree got my attention.

Bottom left: This was one of the bridges that had been condemned by the Forest Service.

Above: These bighorn sheep had come down from the mountains to graze. This was my actual campsite.

Middle: This is a picture of the ram just as he started to attack me.

Bottom: This picture was taken several minutes and about three trees later. At this point, he felt safe and I felt exhausted.

After the three-ring main event, the rest of the herd played Follow the Leader.

You turn and look back down the mountain road that brought you, but sounds of visitors do not follow. Except for the stream and the wind in the pines, there are no noises. The only things coming from the buildings are shadows and, maybe for some, memories.

The campground, road, and vacation ranch are wholly located in the Shoshone National Forest. Summer would obviously be the best time of the year to visit.

WALCOTT (Carbon)

Walcott is one of a number of cast-off Union Pacific railroad towns strung out along the old Lincoln Highway. A study of various maps shows Walcott in three different locations. Here's why. First, there are two Walcotts. Second, maps are often wrong. One location is shown to be at the I-80/Highway 30 interchange. This is technically new Walcott. It consists of a gas station and a partially abandoned mobile home park. Another location is shown to be inside the curve these two roads form, that is, slightly southeast of Highway 30 and north of I-80. This is incorrect. The third location is shown to be about a mile northwest of new Walcott. Visible from Highway 30, this is the correct location of the ghost town.

This is new Walcott that is next to the interstate. Over half of it is vacant.

If you need directions, just ask at the only gas station at the #235 interchange. After exiting I-80, drive north on Highway 30 for only a couple hundred yards and take the first road on the left. This is Carbon County Road 215. It is a dirt road but still fine for the family vehicle during dry conditions.

Above: This is part of the old location of Walcott. The buildings in the background belong to a ranch. A couple of the sheds date from the old boom days.

Below: This was the Glub Saloon. It is now part of a rancher's front yard.

Walcott probably got started when the railroad first came through during the 1860s. Between 1890 and 1910, it was one of the busiest railroad shipping centers in the West. Today, it is a sheep station. While at its peak, it shipped ore and timber from Medicine Bow and cattle and sheep from the plain. Mining equipment, building materials, and immigrants were hauled in. There was a hotel, two livery stables, a railroad depot, and a number of stores and saloons. During the mining boom, its population topped at several hundred. The Union Pacific rail line bisected the town. Several dirt roads spoked off in different directions from this transportation point.

In 1908, when the copper boom went bust, Walcott's economy took a hit. The timber industry overtimbered the Medicine Bow Mountains and rapidly declined. The Lincoln Highway was built and missed the town by one mile. The end came in 1940 when the railroad company removed the depot. I do not know when the last citizens left here, but sometime before the 1970s, the Viviam Sheep Company bought the north side of town and converted all the buildings into a sheep station. It was still a sheep station on my visit in the summer of 2002.

There are numerous original buildings, but it is a working station and viewing must be confined to the south side of the tracks. On the southern side of the tracks are two original buildings, both on posted private property. One is on top of a hill and barely in view. The second is the Glub Saloon (at least that's what the sign says). Wholly intact and complete with false front, it is right next to the road and easily viewable. Its name faded badly over time but is still visible. The old saloon is highly photographical.

The front entrance to the saloon is a double door, but the doors don't match. The false front shows evidence of having more than one name. The "s" in saloon is backwards. The previous owner's name was still visible above the word saloon in the 1970s but has since faded. It said "John H. Lewis" and the "s" wasn't backwards. This saloon used to be on the main street of town. The railroad that splits this old community is active; watch for trains.

This is the remainder of old Walcott. Now a sheep station, it is located north of the Union Pacific tracks.

WELCOME (Crook)

The welcome mat is not out in Welcome, a town located in a very remote and beautiful part of the Black Hills National Forest. Arsonists, litterers, souvenir hunters, thieves, and vandals have made others unwelcome in parts of the Black Hills, including this town.

The ironic thing is that so many books use it as a point of reference. If these books send you to Tinton, Mineral, etc., they send you via Welcome. Some even suggest you ask for directions here. Good luck; there is usually nobody to ask. Also, Welcome only appears on a few National Forest maps.

Welcome's history is sketchy. It was a service mining town during both the gold and tin rushes. In 1904, the Golden Empire Mining Company built a twenty-stamp mill here to serve the gold mines of Mineral Hill. The Black Hills Tin Company also operated here at one time.

The road to Welcome is rough even in good weather. I hiked it.

This restored house is the last completely intact structure in Welcome.

Welcome is situated along Sand Creek. The remains consist of one intact two-story log residence, the ruins of three others, an old pump house, and an ore cart. There was a Forest Service sign that said "Welcome," but on my last visit, it was missing. Most likely, souvenir hunters stole the sign. The owners of the only occupied residence in Welcome hoped the Forest Service would replace it. This residence was recently rebuilt. The building had to be lifted intact so that a foundation could be placed underneath it. The house had been built so well that the shell had outlasted the original wood and stone floor joists. German carpenters, who obviously knew their work, built it. There is a 1920s shed behind the house, and the ore cart is in the front yard.

A dog charged at me, but it turned out to be a friendly charge. The dog's name was Rose, and she accompanied me to the next ghost town of Mineral Hill. She was a very nice mid-afternoon companion—even stopping with me during a lunch break.

Sources have their preferred routes to this site. All agree that whichever route you take, it's a hard travel. Tinton, Mineral Hill, and the South Dakota border are all within a couple of miles. Summer is the best time to visit; winter or bad weather can make roads impassable. To find Welcome, you need the correct topographic or National Forest map and the ability to follow it. Be aware, the National Forest map has some inaccuracies. It shows a road passing in front of Welcome, but it no longer does. Now there is a fence and a small pond where the map says there's a road. Instead, a road goes around and behind Welcome on its approach to Mineral Hill. This road is not depicted on the map.

On your way to and at Mineral Hill, you will see more roads and trails that are also not marked on the National Forest map. This is a good and very useful map, but do not consider it to be flawless. Such thinking about any map can get you into a lot of trouble. Weather is always a factor. Lack of visibility can keep you from seeing important terrain features. The morning I started this hike, the fog kept visibility to about twenty feet. I stuck to the roads, and the sun burnt off the morning mist by about nine o'clock.

If you are fortunate enough to meet the only family in Welcome, be nice to them because they are nice people. They will tell you which boards on the ground denote the old post office. They provided a wealth of information and directions, treated me to a viewing of a scrapbook on the history of the area, and were Rose's owners.

WINTON (Sweetwater)
SITE NOT VISITED

Winton was a coal-mining town that was abandoned in the 1950s. Conditions of its remains are unknown to me. The route to Winton is a dirt road, and its condition varies greatly with the weather. There are other challenges to driving here. It's a maze of roads and easy to get lost. High sand dunes traverse the area, blocking roads at a whim. Its approximate location is ten miles northwest of Rock Springs. Follow State Highway 191 north to the Reliance road. Turn

Sheep, not just cattle, are important to the Wyoming livestock industry and history.

right here, and then left on the Winton road. Follow this road north until you reach Road 18, aka the Superior Cutoff. A mile or two down the cutoff is a road spur that heads northeast. This is the road to Winton. A railroad spur parallels the road to the location.

At its peak, Winton had six mines and hundreds of structures, including the company store, a boardinghouse, a pool hall, a doctor's office, a school, a tipple, a bathhouse, the post office, and the mine office. Main Street ran east to west, but the rest of the town was laid out in a hodgepodge fashion. The Union Pacific Railroad ran a feeder line to the town. Warning: The environment is harsh; this is not a place to get lost or stuck.

BIBLIOGRAPHY

Even though this is a complete list of ghost town books used for this project, it is still a partial bibliography. Every possible source—website, map, tourist pamphlet, highway historical marker, or park brochure—was used. Information was gleaned from magazine and newspaper articles, postcards, and such unique sources as restaurant placemats. Interviews with local postmasters, mayors, business owners, and even people just wandering into camp have been integrated into this book. In addition, two different PBS specials provided information. But the most important research came from personally visiting as many of the towns and cemeteries as I could. These personal visits furnished the majority of the information for this book.

Backcountry Treks. Discovery Travel Adventures. Bethesda, MD: Discovery Communications, 2000.

Florin, Lambert. *Ghost Towns of the West*. [New York]: Promontory Press, 1971.

———. *Western Ghost Towns*. Seattle: Superior Publishing Co., 1961.

Off the Beaten Path. Pleasantville, NY: Reader's Digest Association, 1987.

Parker, Watson, and Hugh K. Lambert. *Black Hills Ghost Towns*. Chicago: Swallow Press, 1974.

Pence, Mary Lou, and Lola M. Homsher. *The Ghost Towns of Wyoming*. New York: Hastings House, 1956.

Radeka, Lynn, and Gary Topping. *Ghost Towns of the Old West*. New York: Mallard Press, 1992.

Wallace, Robert. *The Miners*. Edited by the editors of Time-Life Books. New York: Time-Life, 1976.

Weis, Norman D. *Ghost Towns of the Northwest*. Caldwell, ID: Caxton Printers, 1971.

Wild West. Discovery Travel Adventures. Bethesda, MD: Discovery Communications, 1999.

Wolle, Muriel Sibell. *The Bonanza Trail: Ghost Towns and Mining Camps of the West*. Bloomington: Indiana University Press, 1953.

Wyoming Atlas & Gazetteer. Yarmouth, ME: DeLorme Mapping, 2001.

ABOUT THE AUTHOR

Bruce A. Raisch, ghost town hunter, historian, and photographer, was born with the love for outdoor adventure. On his western trips, some of the activities he enjoys are canyoneering, extreme hiking, horseback riding, solo mountain climbing, and whitewater rafting.

He has earned a Bachelor of Science in Business Administration and served with the United States Army in Saudi Arabia and Kuwait for Operation Desert Shield. Currently he resides in St. Louis, Missouri.

To learn more about the author, visit his website, www.theghosttownhunter.com, or email him at bar4916@yahoo.com.

Bruce A. Raisch at Yellowstone Canyon.